Designed and produced by
Albany Books
36 Park Street London W1Y 4DE

Published in the United States of America
by Galahad Books
95 Madison Avenue New York
New York 10016

First impression 1981

House Editor: Gwen Rigby
Art Direction: Elizabeth Cooke
Design: Pauline Harrison

ISBN 0-88365-550-0
Library of Congress Catalog Card Number: 81-80489

Text photoset 12/14 pt Baskerville 169
by SX Composing Limited, Rayleigh, Essex

Printed and bound in Spain by Printer Industria Gráfica SA.

DLB 3977 1981

Endpapers
Members of the *corps de ballet* of the Tokyo Ballet Company
in *Palais de Cristal* by Balanchine

Half-title
Baryshnikov and Makarova dancing in *Giselle*

Title page
John Cranko based his ballet *Eugene Onegin* on the poem by
Pushkin, and it is now in the repertoire of many ballet
companies. Here Anthony Dowell and Antoinette Sibley
dance in the Royal Ballet production

Contents page
Suzanne Farrell and Jorge Donn in Béjart's ballet
Nijinsky, Clown de Dieu

World
Ballet

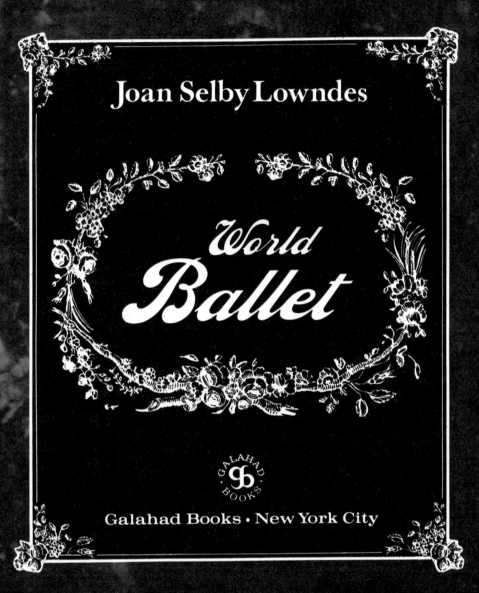

Joan Selby Lowndes

World
Ballet

Galahad Books · New York City

Contents

1
Early History

Though dancing is as old as man, the first glimpse of ballet as we know it today is in the Italian courts at the time of the Renaissance, when elaborate spectacles of singing, poetry and dancing were staged.

The Italian *balletto*, meaning 'little dance', travelled to France where it became *le ballet*, and was taken over by the French court. Italian dancing masters began passing on to their French pupils an art and technique that had already become highly polished.

One of the more promising pupils was a 12-year-old boy who also happened to be King of France. Young Louis developed a passion for dancing and the theatre very early on in his life; at thirteen he made his début, dancing before the court, and two years later he was the central figure in a magnificent entertainment *Le Ballet de la Nuit* in which he appeared as the Sun round whom the whole civilized world revolves. The year was 1653 and with Louis XIV, 'the Sun King', the story of French ballet begins.

So long as Louis himself continued to perform, ballet remained the exclusive property of the nobility. Royal palaces were the settings for huge, elaborate productions, usually with classical Greek or Roman themes, in which courtiers dressed in extravagant costumes and headdresses. Two men were responsible for mounting these spectacles: Beauchamp and Lully.

Pierre Beauchamp was the king's ballet master, and his task was the 'choreography'. He did not have much scope for his work as dancing, hampered by heavy costumes, high heels and ideas of decorum, consisted mainly of stately measures in which the dancers progressed in geometrical patterns across

King Sun was recreated by Anton Dolin in the 1950s for the Festival Ballet. The elaborate feathered headdress of this costume started a fashion in the French theatre that survives to this day with the dancers of the Folies Bergères revues. (*Mike Davis Studios, Jesse Davis*)

The most famous role of fourteen-year-old King Louis XIV of France was King Sun (*Le roi soleil*) in the *Ballet de la Nuit*. The ballet began at sunset and went on through thirteen hours of darkness to culminate at dawn with the appearance of King Sun in this magnificent costume. It was also the dawn of Louis's long and great reign and, in consequence, he came to be called '*Le roi soleil*'. (*Mander & Mitchenson Theatre Collection*)

the floor, with elegant arm and head movements, and feet nicely turned out to show off silver buckles or ribbons.

Beauchamp, who took a deep and intelligent interest in dancing technique, worked to improve this by introducing more natural movements. The story goes that he kept pigeons in the loft of his house and used always to feed them himself because, watching their movements and the groups they formed as they pecked up the grain, gave him ideas for his dances. The result (uninfluenced by pigeon toes) was a great advance in dancing standards, and Beauchamp is credited with having established the basic 'five positions' of classical ballet.

He was also one of the first to work on an ingenious system of dance notation to record movement, but his idea was pirated by Raoul-Auger Feuillet, who in 1700 published *Choreography, or the Art of Describing the Dance*

Beauchamp's colleague Jean Baptiste Lully, was the showman and organizer. This lively urchin from Florence, had come to the French court as a 14-year-old page, and made himself noticed through his

talent for comedy and music. Young King Louis, who was a quick talent spotter, soon appointed him Master of the Royal Music, and the ambitious Lully took over the production of the court spectacles.

For nearly twenty years Lully and Beauchamp satisfied the king's passion for dancing and appearing as a star performer. The dangerous moment came when Louis, at the age of thirty, realized he was getting stout and had the good sense to retire. Fortunately, a rising young dramatist Molière had been entertaining the court with his plays, and Lully and Beauchamp teamed up with him to produce a new type of spectacle that combined dancing and acting. They had immediate success, first with *Les Fâcheux* and then, in 1670, with the most famous entertainment of them all *Le Bourgeois Gentilhomme*. This was the beginning of the move away from productions by the amateur dancers of the court towards those by a new generation of professionals in the theatre.

Here again, Louis XIV helped. In 1672 he gave Lully a charter to found *L'Academie Royale de la Musique*; this was the birth of the Paris Opéra we know today.

It began life in an old converted tennis court near the Luxembourg Palace, and here Lully and Beauchamp put on their first shows in a place that was so rickety it threatened to fall apart. Fortunately it held together for a few months, when Molière

The five basic positions of classical ballet were said to have been established by Pierre Beauchamp, who was King Louis's ballet master. He founded the first official school of ballet in 1672, and did most of the choreography for the court spectaculars and for the emerging professional theatre ballets. (*Mike Davis Studios, Jesse Davis*)

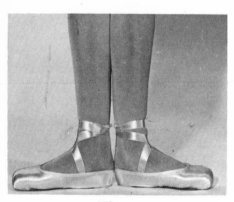

First

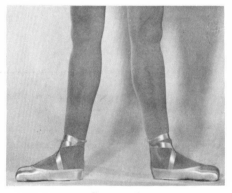

Second

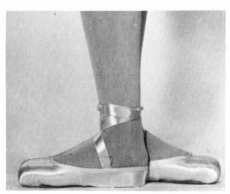

Third

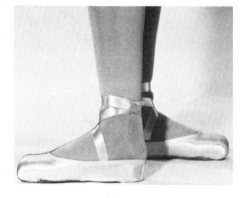

Fourth open

Fourth closed

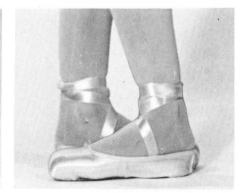

Fifth

Le Triomphe de l'Amour is a milestone in ballet history. First produced as a court spectacular in 1681, it was transferred to the stage of the Palais Royal. Here, for the first time, professional femal dancers appeared. There were four of them – seen in the foreground of this picture – led by Mlle de la Fontaine, in the centre, who became the first 'ballerina'. The elaborate architectural set is typical of the period. (*Mansell Collection*)

LEFT Marie-Thérèse Subligny became the second ballerina of the Paris Opéra at the time when the fashion for face patches was at its height. She was usually partnered by Jean Balon, favourite dancer of the ageing King Louis, and was the first professional ballerina to appear in England, between 1700 and 1702. (*Mary Evans Picture Library*)

unexpectedly died, and the astute Lully quickly manoeuvred himself and his Academy into the premises occupied by Molière's troupe of actors in the Palais Royal.

Though a royal palace sounded a grand address, the Academy's part of it was a gloomy place at the end of a *cul de sac*, looking more like a prison than a theatre, with a long, narrow, badly-lit auditorium

13

encrusted with dirt. This, however, was to be the home of the Paris Opéra for the next ninety years until, mercifully, it burned down, and here Beauchamp founded the first school of ballet. He was a great teacher. Precision, elegance and nobility were the hallmarks he imprinted on his dancers, setting a style that has been part of French ballet tradition ever since.

His first pupils were all men, for there was no question of female dancers appearing on the professional stage at that time, their roles were taken by boys. A situation which was made possible by the fact that all dancers wore masks – a curious survival of a custom that went back to the days of classical Greek drama, and had been perpetuated by the Italian Commedia dell' arte.

It was not until the dance evolved as a complete art form in its own right during the next century, that masks finally disappeared. In the meantime, a first move in this direction was made in 1681 when Lully and Beauchamp presented a new Opera-Ballet, *Le Triomphe de l'Amour*. For the first time, dancing had a really important part and, for the first time also, female dancers appeared – four of them! Their leader was the tall, statuesque Mlle de la Fontaine, whose grace and elegance earned her the title, 'Queen of the Dance'. She continued to reign at the Paris Opéra for twelve years and then retired, surprisingly, to become a nun.

By this time Lully was dead, Beauchamp had retired and his pupil Louis Pécour, was ballet master. Star performers now began to appear. One of the brightest was young Jean Balon, famous for his lightness and elevation. He was well named for *ballon*, a ball, came to be the technical term for a dancer's springiness and skill in jumping.

The great star of the new century, however, was Louis Dupré, who made his début as a young man of eighteen in 1715. Tall and elegant, with a magnificent physique and a powerful stage presence, he dominated the scene for the next forty years. Casanova has left us a vivid description of the ageing 'Grand Dupré' on stage, wearing a waist length black wig and a mask, yet able to captivate his audience by the sheer perfection of his movements as a *danseur noble*. Social distinctions from the days of court dancing still clung to the professional theatre. Dancers were graded into the aristocratic *danseur noble*; the pure character dancer *demi-caractère*, or the lowest type, the *danseur comique*. Soloists coming out of the *corps de ballet* were usually type-cast for life in one of these ranks.

This was a world of male dancers who continued to dominate the scene as they developed their technique. Females were having a much more difficult time because of the long skirts that hid their legs and made advanced footwork and jumping impossible. It was not until new fashions came in with the new king Louis XV that their chance came. It was seized with both hands by a lively young dancer called Marie Camargo.

This fiery 16-year-old beauty, said to be of noble Spanish and Italian descent, made a spectacular début one night in 1726 when a male dancer missed his cue and she took the stage, dancing his variation so brilliantly that she scored a triumph.

Her teacher, Dupré's partner Mlle Prévost, was furious, but a tearful Marie was taken on as a pupil by Nicholas Blondy, nephew of Beauchamp and a magnificent dancer. Later Le Grand Dupré himself taught her. She was lucky. Under male teachers she developed her ability to jump and to do beaten steps such as an *entrechat quatre*, which no woman had performed in Paris before. Marie Camargo had speed, skill and gaiety. She also dared to shorten her skirts to the ankles, and she became the toast of Paris.

She did not have it all her own way, however, for there was a rival, Marie Sallé, who also had a big following. No two dancers could have presented a greater contrast. Sallé came from a family troupe of itinerant French actors. Her father was an acrobat and she had begun her career as a 9-year-old child prodigy dancing in a pantomime at the Lincolns Inn Fields Theatre in London.

Not far away in the Drury Lane Theatre, John Weaver was making ballet history at this time with his *Loves of Mars and Venus* which is the earliest known *ballet d'action*. That is to say, Weaver had done away with words and songs: the dancers themselves told the story with mime and gesture. It could well be that the child, Marie Sallé, saw this ballet while she was in London, and that it influenced her ideas, for she too became a pioneer of the *ballet d'action*. Back in Paris she went on to study under Mlle Prévost making her début at the Opéra a year after Camargo. Marie Sallé developed into a dancer of great dramatic sensitivity.

Where Camargo excited audiences with her technical brilliance, Marie Sallé charmed them with her delicate grace and the moving eloquence of her mime. While Camargo's love affairs provided fuel for the gossips of Paris, Sallé presented a picture of a model of virtue, though there were rumours that she was a lesbian. She was, however, daring enough to appear at London's Covent Garden in the

Mlle Camargo Dancing by Nicolas Lancret. At the age of 16 this lively virtuoso dancer became a star performer at the Paris Opéra. Her artistry did much to advance ballet technique for women dancers and she was also a leader of the new fashion for lighter, shorter skirts, lifting hers above the ankles to show off her brilliant footwork. (*London, Wallace Collection*)

classical *Pygmalion*, wearing transparent Greek draperies and sandals, and with unbound hair. It caused a sensation. David Garrick the actor recalled that people were fighting to get into the theatre that night!

Sallé was not, in fact, a sensationalist, she was a creative, dramatic dancer living ahead of her time. Her ideas had a strong influence on one young admirer 13-year-old Jean Noverre, who was a pupil at the Paris Opéra ballet school under the great Dupré. Noverre quickly realized that the Dupré style of dancing was out of date, and he had the nerve to describe his famous master as a machine – a perfect and beautiful machine with no soul, for whatever role he danced he always remained Dupré.

For Noverre, as for Sallé, the soul of the dance was what mattered. Noverre believed with all the ardour of a missionary that ballet should be a complete drama, in which dancing should be based on character and situation, and not meaningless entertainment or personal display. Years ahead of his time, Noverre believed in a close relationship between movement and music, action and décor. As a logical consequence he fought to liberate dancers from the inhibiting trappings of fashion. He

Marie Sallé made her first appearance at the Paris Opéra in 1727 and became the great rival to Camargo. Her talent, in complete contrast, was as a dramatic dancer of great power. She was able deeply to move her audiences with the charm and eloquence of her dancing. This engraving is after a painting, also by Lancret. (*Mary Evans Picture Library*)

wanted to see their costumes designed for freedom of movement to enable them to express the characters they portrayed.

Noverre was not the only person thinking along these lines. The rapid advance in the technique of dancing had already led to a demand for greater opportunities of expression. It was Noverre, however, who formulated these ideas into a book, *Letters on Dancing and Ballet* published in 1760. It has become a classic, and most of the basic principles in it are still valid today. It was largely due to Noverre that the function of the choreographer was raised from the hack work of arranging steps to fit so many bars of music, to a creative level as the power centre of a ballet production.

Noverre's first opportunity to try out his ideas had come in 1751, when he staged a remarkable ballet *Les Fêtes Chinoises* in Lyons. Its tremendous success led to a Paris production, and from there he was invited by David Garrick to stage his ballet in London's Drury Lane.

Unfortunately politics interfered. Anti-French feeling was running high at the time, there were riots in the theatre, and the ballet had to be withdrawn. One happy result, however, was a lasting friendship between Noverre and Garrick, who called him 'The Shakespeare of the Dance'. It seems likely that most of Noverre's ideas on mime in ballet were learned from the great actor.

It was in Stuttgart that Noverre was able to do his finest work. The wealthy, theatre-loving Duke Charles II of Württemburg, invited him to form a ballet company in 1760, in seven years Noverre built up a trained company of fifty dancers, produced many of his best works and turned Stuttgart into a major ballet centre, where most of the leading dancers of the day appeared.

By now the great explosion of ballet across Europe was under way. Dancers and ballet masters were circulating through all the great cities of Europe where royal opera houses were opening their doors to them. They must have had incredible stamina, for travelling conditions in those days of horse-drawn transport were diabolical. They had to endure rough roads, iron-tyred vehicles on swaying springs, damp and dubious hostelries for overnight stops, the permanent risk of being held up by highwaymen, and an average travelling speed of ten miles per hour. Yet, surprisingly enough, a look at the life span of the leading figures shows that most of them far outlived the contemporary average life expectation of forty years, and survived into their seventies and eighties. Indeed, Noverre, who lived to be 83, spent the first ten years of his dancing career appearing in Berlin, Dresden, Strasbourg, Marseilles and Lyons. By the time he reached Stuttgart, however, he had more or less abandoned dancing for choreography.

His success in Stuttgart led to an invitation to take charge of the ballet at the Royal Opera House in Vienna. The way for Noverre and his ideas had already been prepared by Vienna's great ballet master Franz Hilverding, who had established a well-trained company and pioneered *ballets d'action*. When he moved on to St. Petersburg in 1758, his favourite pupil Italian-born Angiolini had taken over and continued to develop his master's idea.

Angiolini's best-known work was *Don Juan*, for which the composer Gluck wrote an enchanting score. Angiolini claimed that this was the first ballet-pantomime based on ancient Greek and Roman mimes. *Don Juan* was so popular that it remained in the repertoire for forty years, and influenced many contemporary choreographers. A remarkable revival by Fokine in 1936 for the Ballets

Russes in London started a whole series of new versions. So, the old story and music live on in the hands of modern choreographers.

The fiery Angiolini resented Noverre's claim to be the originator of the *ballets d'action* and the quarrel grew to epic proportions. In fact, the basis of the disagreement was not who started the *ballets d'action* but which way the new development should go. Angiolini, who liked taut, concentrated action in his ballets, supported the contemporary convention of the three unities. These were the rules governing plays, which demanded a single plot, a single set, with action taking place in a single unit of time. Noverre claimed that this did not apply to ballet. In the end, of course, time proved him right, as the unities have long ceased to apply to either drama or ballet.

A more controversial point, however, was Angiolini's hatred of printed programme notes. Noverre liked to publish an outline of his ballet stories to help the audience; Angiolini claimed that good dance and mime should make this unnecessary. The argument still goes on!

In a sense, both men were right with regard to their own talents. Angiolini had the skill to choose stories that could be easily understood in mime. Noverre, on the other hand, tended to choose complex dramas that depended on words. As a result, none of his ballets has lived, but what has survived are his *Letters on Dancing and Ballet*, which he spent his life revising and re-editing. His far-seeing ideas were not only a powerful influence on his contemporaries, but have lived on in the works of succeeding generations of choreographers.

Among those he influenced by personal contact was Gaetan Vestris, who had travelled regularly to Stuttgart to appear as a guest artist in Noverre's ballets. Gaetan was the new star of the Paris Opéra where he had been a pupil of the Grand Dupré, who had retired at last.

Paris was now applauding brilliant dancing in an entirely new style for Gaetan Vestris had far outgrown his master. He brought to the stately French *danseur noble* tradition the speed and liveliness of his Italian theatrical ancestry. Such jumping and pirouettes had never been seen before. The public began by admiring his beautiful legs and ended by bestowing on him the accolade of *Le dieu de la danse*, a very rare honour.

On stage he was truly a god; off stage he was impossibly conceited and insufferably arrogant. It is probably due to his vanity that he was one of the first dancers to appear without a mask in his own ballet *Medea and Jason* in 1771. This was one of the new Noverre-type *ballets d'action*, and Gaetan, in the leading role of Jason, discarded the mask so as to give full scope for his facial expressions. Many of the audience seeing a dancer bare-faced for the first time were genuinely shocked.

They were in for a further shock the following year when another leading dancer, Maximilien Gardel, also appeared on stage without a mask. His reason was so as not to be mistaken for Gaetan whose role he had taken over. At long last Noverre's ideas had broken through the outworn convention. After this, masks were rapidly relegated to history and the museums.

That same year 1772 also marked the début of a 12-year-old boy. Proudly introduced by his father

Gaetan Vestris was born in Florence in 1728 and died in Paris in 1808. This handsome, talented and insufferably conceited man triumphed at the Paris Opéra for years. His brilliant artistry combined the stately French style of court dancing, with the speed and elevation of the more lively Italian tradition. He was the first dancer to appear on stage without a mask. (*London, Victoria and Albert Museum*)

The clog dance from *La Fille Mal Gardée* is one of the most popular *divertissements*. Sir Frederick Ashton based his choreography for this on the traditional Lancashire clog dance. (*Mike Davis Studios, Jesse Davis*)

LEFT *La Fille Mal Gardée* is one of the oldest surviving ballets. Created by Jean Dauberval of the Paris Opéra, it had its premiere in Bordeaux in July 1798, only a few days before the outbreak of the French Revolution. It was the first ballet to break with the tradition of classical gods and heroes, bringing the story into the homely setting of a French farm. The production shown here was choreographed by Sir Frederick Ashton for the Royal Ballet. The Maypole Dance captures the light-hearted summer spirit of harvest time, that has made this ballet popular all over the world. (*Mike Davis Studios, Jesse Davis*)

as a child prodigy, young Auguste Vestris danced in public for the first time, giving a performance that showed all the future promise of a brilliant dancer. Fortunately, the conceited Gaetan took all the credit for his son's talents on himself, and was not jealous. In fact Auguste had inherited his gifts from both his parents, for his mother Marie Allard, who had been one of Gaetan's mistresses, was a talented young dancer at the Opéra, much admired for her lightness and brilliance in character and comedy roles.

The Vestris, father and son, were to dominate the Paris Opéra until Gaetan retired in 1782 at the age of 55. Auguste was then 22 and at the height of his powers. Although he was rather short and inclined to be knock-kneed, his footwork, elevation and the speed of his pirouettes were sensational. He was also a very expressive dancer and the public honoured

Auguste Vestris (1760–1842) was the illegitimate son of Gaetan Vestris and the dancer Marie Allard. He inherited his parents' talents, and grew up to outshine them both, becoming not only the greatest dancer of his day, but a key figure in ballet history as a teacher. Passing on the artistry and technique he had developed so brilliantly, he influenced a whole new generation of dancers. (*London, Victoria and Albert Museum*)

RIGHT Emilie Bigottini was a ballerina of the Paris Opéra, much admired for her dramatic style, who became one of Napoleon's favourite dancers. She is seen here dancing in the premiere of *Cinderella*, partnered by François Albert, who did the choreography for this production. (*London, Victoria and Albert Museum*)

him with his father's title *Le dieu de la dance*, which simply reinforced his egocentricity for he was as vain as Gaetan. For thirty-six years he reigned over the Paris Opéra. Though his dancing achievement was of key importance in the development of ballet, his greatest contribution was as a teacher, for he was able to pass his knowledge on to his pupils and most of the great dancers of the next generation passed through his hands.

While the Vestris's dancing brought the technique of ballet to new heights of brilliance, Noverre's ideas on choreography were taking root all over Europe as the great explosion of ballet sent dancers and ballet masters circulating through the big cities. Berlin and Vienna, Copenhagen, Sweden and Milan all formed ballet companies at this time, and many built splendid new opera houses. Even provincial cities followed the trend. In south-west France, Bordeaux opened its Grand Théâtre in 1780 and shortly afterwards a new ballet master, Jean Dauberval, arrived from Paris.

Trained by Dupré, he had been a soloist at the Opéra for some time and was a fine dancer, but his real genius lay in choreography. He had been deeply influenced by Noverre, and now he had the opportunity that in Paris had been denied him. He put Bordeaux's new theatre on the map with a series of brilliant *ballets d'action*, the most famous of which is *La Fille Mal Gardée*.

First produced in 1789, this ballet reflects a whole new style of thinking. Dauberval had replaced the old classical gods and heroes with a story of ordinary people. His purpose, he said, was 'to interest the heart as well as to please the eye'.

La Fille Mal Gardée takes the ballet out of its usual palace setting and puts it into a homely French farm at harvest time. Lise the pretty, high-spirited daughter of the house, runs rings round her poor old mother Widow Simone, who scolds and threatens and tries to force her wilful daughter into marriage with Alain, the son of a suitably wealthy vineyard owner. But Lise is in love with the handsome farmhand Colas while Alain is a clown of a youth, trying to please his father and forever doing the wrong thing. Against the merry dancing of the young harvesters, the plot resolves itself into a lovers' intrigue which eventually ends happily when the lovers are forgiven and united. This colourful, charming ballet has been through the hands of many choreographers since its premiere and is still a favourite with ballet goers.

It was the first ballet created for ordinary people, and Dauberval produced it at just the right time, for the ordinary people were about to seize power. The country was seething with underground pressures and, within weeks of the ballet's premiere, the explosion came. On 14 July 1789, the Paris mob stormed the Bastille, that grim prison which was for them a symbol of the cruel power of the kings of France.

It was the beginning of a ten-year upheaval. The leaders of the Revolution struggled among themselves for power, culminating in the blood bath of the 'reign of terror' when the French people killed their king and queen and hunted down every aristocrat they could find, to bring to the guillotine. It was not until Napoleon seized power in 1799 that order was restored and the French, having destroyed the dictatorship of their kings, thankfully accepted the dictatorship of the Emperor Napoleon Bonaparte.

Through all this the Paris Opéra managed to survive, thanks to the courage, skill and diplomacy of one man, Pierre Gardel the chief ballet master, who had taken over the post in 1787 when his elder brother Maximilien had died very suddenly from an infected toe. When the revolution came many dancers fled, including Auguste Vestris who took refuge in England. Pierre Gardel, however, remained loyally at his post. Adapting himself and his theatre to a rapidly changing world, he managed to win and keep the approval of the revolutionary authorities, and none of his dancers went to the guillotine. He continued in favour with Napoleon, who even strengthened the monopoly of the Opéra by closing some rival theatres. When the Bonaparte Empire was swept away, Pierre Gardel survived under the restoration, and found favour with the new constitutional monarch Louis XVIII.

By this time, Gardel was virtually the dictator of the Opéra, but he used his power to give the dancers security and the opportunity of continuing artistic development. It was a time of great dancers. Auguste Vestris had returned to shine more brightly than ever, despite a rival who had sprung up in his absence Louis Duport, a much younger man whose lithe grace dazzled his audiences.

Though male dancers still dominated the scene, there were now some powerful ballerinas, such as Anne Heinel from Germany and Marie Gardel, Pierre's wife.

What Pierre Gardel did not do was to give opportunities to choreographers. He liked to hold the reins of power in his own hands and almost every ballet production was his own creation. It was from the hands of Dauberval in Bordeaux that the new generation of choreographers was emerging.

Charles Didelot, who had trained under him in Paris and made his début under Noverre, had already made his mark in London with *Flore et Zéphire*, and was now away in St. Petersburg, bringing dramatic ballet to the Russians.

Italian, Salvatore Viganó was deeply influenced by Dauberval and worked with him for a time before going on to fame in Vienna and Milan, where he became ballet master at La Scala and gave the theatre its greatest triumphs with his brilliant choreography.

Carlo Blasis also studied with Dauberval in Paris and Bordeaux and went on to become a soloist at La Scala under Viganò. Although he worked as a choreographer, his real fame was as a teacher. When an injury brought his dancing career to an end he took over the school at La Scala and made it world famous. His pupils were the brilliant dancers who starred in most of the European theatres and dominated the Russian ballet. Blasis's book, *The Code of Terpsichore*, published in London in 1828 is a teacher's classic, and one of several that he wrote. It is Blasis's work that laid the foundations of the classical dancer's vocabulary today.

By the time Pierre Gardel retired in 1820, after more than thirty years at the Opéra, the dance scene had changed completely. Dramatic ballet was now firmly established and dancers were dressed for their job. Padded breeches, powdered wigs and high heels had vanished, along with masks. Tights and soft flat shoes gave freedom of movement, and the first experiments were being made with dancing on points.

The Opéra itself was making a new start, for that same year, 1820, it moved from the old building to a fine theatre in rue Peletier. The scene was set for the entrance of the Romantic Ballet.

2

Romantic Ballet

On 12 March 1832 the great auditorium of the Paris Opéra filled with a first night audience who had come to see a new ballet *La Sylphide*.

The bright glow of flames from the new gas lighting gleamed on the theatre's gilded carvings and the public's expensive jewellery as wealthy society rustled its programmes and chattered. It was not so long before that the theatre had been lit by candles and oil lamps whose smoke could often obscure the stage, and some people there might even have remembered the first theatre in Paris to be lit by gas more than forty years earlier. An English circus showman Philip Astley had built the Amphithéâtre Anglais in the Faubourg du Temple, and Queen Marie Antoinette herself had been present on the opening night in 1785 when Astley dazzled Paris with the illuminations from twelve thousand jets of gas.

By 1832 most of the theatres were gas lit, which opened up a whole new range of possibilities for scenic designers. It also means that, for the first time, the lights of the auditorium could be dimmed and an audience sitting in semi-darkness could project themselves into the make-believe world of the brightly-lit stage.

This was now the theatre as we know it today. There were even seats for everyone for the old-style walk-about pit had become the stalls with expensive plush seats. The orchestra pit separating the stage from the public had already been in existence for a long time. The musicians tuned up, and there was a hush as the house lights faded.

The curtain rose and the audience found itself in

A contemporary production of *La Sylphide* by the Danish Ballet with Anna Laerkeson in the leading role. (*Mike Davis Studios, Jesse Davis*)

Scotland, in the sombre interior of a farmhouse. Most of the room was in shadow and the only light seemed to come from the glow of the fire on the wide hearth. A big armchair was drawn up before it and the young farmer James, a solid earthy figure in his tartan kilt and buckled shoes, was asleep unaware of a radiant white figure hovering near him. La Sylphide, attracted by this handsome young man, circled round him. As she danced she seemed to float across the stage and the audience could hardly believe its eyes. The dancer was travelling on the very tips of her toes – on points; and she was doing it with effortless ease. Not only this, but all her movements had a fluid grace that transformed her into a spirit of ethereal beauty. Such dancing had never been seen before, nor had such a costume which was sensational in its simplicity – a soft white dress with a bell-shaped skirt of filmy layers that floated about the dancer's legs as she moved.

Marie Taglioni is seen here in her greatest role as *La Sylphide*, created in 1832. She was the first romantic ballerina; the first dancer to use the new technique of dancing on points with true artistry in a major role; and also the first dancer to wear the simple white costume that has become the hallmark of the ballet dancer. (*London, Victoria and Albert Museum*)

The interior of the Paris Opéra in rue Peletier. The dancers moved into this theatre in 1820 and its stage was the scene of the great romantic ballets. It was totally destroyed by fire in 1873. (*Mary Evans Picture Library*)

This then was Marie Taglioni, the new ballerina of the Opéra. Behind her effortless technique lay years of gruelling hard work under her father's training and ten years of experience on stage under his guidance. The finished product was a young woman who projected an aura of romantic beauty and utter purity, who transformed the act of dancing from mere physical achievement to an expression of sublime poetry. For the audience of 1832 she was the very embodiment of the new romantic ideals of the day.

The story of *La Sylphide* is the love of James for this beautiful creature from the spirit world. He is on the eve of his wedding to Effie, but he abandons her to follow his love into the woods. Here he accepts a magic scarf from the witch, Madge. Believing it will bind his love to him for ever, he places it round her shoulders, but as he holds her in

his arms at last, her wings fall and the beautiful sylphide dies. Far away in the forest the wedding procession of Effie and Gurn, her former suitor, is seen going by. James has lost both his earthly bride and his spirit love. He falls lifeless to the ground.

La Sylphide was a triumph and Marie Taglioni became enshrined in ballet history as the queen of the romantic ballerinas.

Such was the impact of the new ballet that it was seen in London and Berlin within months of its premiere. Vienna saw it in 1836, and that same year August Bournonville staged his own version of it in Copenhagen. In 1837 it was performed in St. Petersburg and crossed the Atlantic to the United States; since then it has been performed all over the world.

Romantic ballet was launched and the Paris Opéra was all set for a great run of success. One of the reasons for the old theatre's new surge of life was a recent change of management. Only the year before, in 1831, the Opéra had been turned into a private enterprise and the new Director Dr. Véron had set about reorganizing the whole place. This

24

clear-thinking, energetic business man, with a flair for showmanship, realized that his prosperity depended on getting the support of the new wealthy middle classes. Box office returns had already shown him what sort of ballets were popular, so he had set out to provide them. An added attraction was his astute plan to allow privileged subscribers back-stage to meet the dancers in the *Foyer* – the French equivalent of the Green Room. This turned the theatre into a sort of exclusive club and the Opéra rapidly became the fashionable gathering place for smart society.

Véron made other changes, sweeping away the old classification of dancers into three socially divisive types – *noble*, *demi-caractère* and *comique* – and instead giving equal opportunities to all dancers

to tackle any role. Another of his more forward-looking moves, anticipating Hollywood film days, was the deliberate creation of the star dancer. Marie Taglioni was his first, and he gave the ancient hierarchy a severe jolt when he promoted this almost unknown performer over the heads of the other dancers and gave her a six-year contract at a fabulous salary.

Two years later he was doing the same thing for another rising young dancer Fanny Elssler, who came from Vienna. The shrewd doctor engaged her as a counter-attraction to Taglioni. He reckoned it would be good for business to have rival ballerinas: he was right. Elssler presented a complete contrast to the ethereal Taglioni. Opinions were soon sharply divided about them and feelings ran high as loyal supporters came to applaud. It was Camargo and Sallé all over again, and business boomed.

Fanny Elssler was the lively earthbound dancer with a powerful personality. While Taglioni's virginal allure aroused deep poetic feelings, Elssler

A rare photograph of the *foyer* or 'green room' of the Paris Opéra, taken about 1860. Privileged subscribers to the Opéra were allowed backstage to meet the dancers, an honour greatly sought after by Parisian society. (*Mary Evans Picture Library*)

charmed her public with her strong dramatic projection and sensual appeal. She was also an extremely competent dancer with speed and attack, able to carry out vigorous movements on her points. It was this development of point work that brought the ballerina to the forefront of the ballet scene, completely eclipsing the male dancer for the

time being. There is no one dancer who can be said to have invented this new technique. It was probably the logical development from dancing on *demi-pointes* to try and balance on the very tip of the toes, and was regarded at first as a purely technical feat, or even a stunt! A Russian dancer Istomina is said to have appeared on points before 1820, and in Paris at about the same time a young French dancer Gosselin achieved an early record of standing on her points for a full minute. It was Taglioni, and Elssler after her, who developed point work as part of a dancer's dramatic vocabulary.

The stage-managed rivalry between the two stars lasted for only a few seasons, but it brought fame to both dancers and a fortune to the astute Dr. Véron who was able to retire after only five years. That same year Taglioni's contract ended and she set off to take romantic ballet to the other capitals of Europe.

Fanny Elssler remained to reign supreme. Not for long however; in 1840 she obtained a year's leave of absence from the Opéra and went to America. She was the first of the new-style ballerinas to cross the Atlantic, and her tour was such a success that she broke her contract with the Opéra and stayed on another year, including Cuba in her itinerary. Her punishment was a heavy fine, but as she had earned a fortune in America this did not worry her, and Paris was the loser for she never danced there again but continued round the European circuit, enjoying one success after another.

In Paris the defection of Fanny Elssler had left the stage denuded of great ballerinas. There was, however, waiting in the wings a rising young star who was to shine even more brightly, perhaps, than her famous predecessors, for she was destined to create the leading role in the most famous romantic ballet of all – *Giselle*.

Carlotta Grisi, born in Italy in 1819, had begun her training at the famous ballet school of La Scala, Milan where she met a French dancer Jules Perrot, who was appearing at Naples. This young man of 23 who had studied under Auguste Vestris, was already making a name for himself as one of the finest dancer-mimes of the day. The teen-age Carlotta Grisi became his pupil, then his mistress, and he launched her career.

Fanny Elssler, the Austrian-born dancer, is seen here in one of her most successful roles as the Spanish dancer in *Le Diable Boîteux*; her *cachucha* solo was a regular show-stopper. She triumphed in Russia as the gipsy girl in *Esmeralda*, and was one of the first European ballerinas to visit the United States where she toured successfully for two years from 1840–1842. (*London, Victoria and Albert Museum*)

The Italian-born dancer Carlotta Grisi created the role of *Giselle* in Paris in 1841. It was to become the greatest classic of the romantic ballets and has since been danced all over the world. (*Mary Evans Picture Library*)

In this young dancer Perrot had the perfect material from which to create a romantic ballerina. Her talents combined those of Elssler and Taglioni for she had the lightness and fluidity of the ethereal dancer, combined with strength and a flair for dramatic projection. She made her Paris début in 1836, but at that time the Taglioni-Elssler rivalry was at its height and no one took much notice of the young Italian girl. She went on to London and Vienna and another five years were to go by before she achieved her ambition and was given a contract with the Opéra as ballerina. Here she met Théophile Gautier, one of the leading romantic poets, who earned his living as a theatre critic and haunted the *Foyer* of the Opéra. Gautier, a true

The Paris Opéra, rue Garnier, which was built in the 1860s by Charles Garnier, became the fifth home of French ballet in 1874 and still is so today. It is claimed that it is the biggest theatre in the world, covering 11,000 square metres. (*Mary Evans Picture Library*)

romantic, worshipped beauty and was highly susceptible to the charms of the dancers. He had already been in love with Taglioni and then with Elssler. He now fell hopelessly in love with Grisi – an unrequited attachment for she preferred her partner Lucien Petipa. It was Grisi, however, who gave Gautier the inspiration for a new ballet *Giselle*, based on an old German legend about the Wilis. It had recently been retold by the German romantic poet Heinrich Heine, who was living in Paris at the time and was a fellow journalist.

Gautier had the good sense to take his idea to a professional librettist Vernoy de Saint-Georges and together they worked out the story of *Giselle* in three days. It was a masterpiece of its time for it cleverly blended the various strands of contemporary romantic feeling: there was the rustic scene expressing the idea of life close to nature held by Jean-Jaques Rousseau; the macabre attractions of the graveyard which appeared in the immensely popular novels of Charles Dickens; the handsome

The story is set in Germany, in the Rhine valley. Giselle, a peasant girl, loves Albrecht unaware that he is a nobleman's son or that he is engaged to Bathilde, the daughter of a duke. Albrecht loves Giselle in return but he has a rival, Hilarion the game-keeper, who is fiercely jealous. At a hunting picnic Hilarion reveals to Giselle the true identity of her lover. The shock is so severe that the young girl loses her reason and dies.

Act II is set at Giselle's lonely tomb where Hilarion and Albrecht come to mourn their lost love. But as midnight sounds the Wilis appear, led by their terrible queen Myrtha. These spirits of young brides who have died before their wedding day because their lovers have been faithless, return to earth each night to take their revenge by luring young men to their death. The beautiful Giselle is now one of them. Hilarion is driven to his death, but Giselle tries to save Albrecht by dancing with him until the dawn comes and the power of the Wilis is broken. The spirits fade into the shadows and Giselle sinks slowly back into her grave, leaving Albrecht stretched motionless on the ground, and the audience guessing whether he is alive or dead. In the original production he was alive and re-united with Bathilde, but this scene has long since disappeared from the ballet.

Jules Perrot, watercolour by A. Charlemagne, 1861. This French-born dancer became the leading soloist at the King's Theatre, London and at the Paris Opéra. He was the teacher, partner and lover of Carlotta Grisi, and created most of her solos in *Giselle*. His great contribution was as a choreographer, his work including *La Esmeralda*, and *Ondine*. (*Moscow, Bakrushin Theatre Museum/Novosti Press Agency*)

hero in the style of Lord Byron and pathetic madness in the Ophelia tradition.

The new director of the Paris Opéra gave the book his blessing, and the ballet went into production with the further blessing of a fine score by a rising young French composer Adolphe Adam, who had a great talent for descriptive music.

The sets were by the top man of the day Ciceri, who had been the chief designer of the Opéra for years and had been responsible for installing gas lighting there in 1822. He had become a past master at using it to create scenic atmosphere.

The choreography of *Giselle* was credited to Jean Coralli the official ballet master, but it seems fairly certain that all Giselle's solos were created for Grisi by Perrot, as they bear the hallmark of a far superior talent. The premiere of *Giselle* took place on 28 June 1841 with Grisi partnered by Lucien Petipa in the leading roles.

Théophile Gautier the writer, poet and theatre critic, was one of the leading influences of the romantic movement in France. He created *Giselle* in collaboration with Vernoy de Saint-Georges, and married the sister of the ballerina Carlotta Grisi. (*Mary Evans Picture Library*)

LEFT Fanny Cerrito was born in Italy and became one of the great romantic ballerinas. She is seen here in *Ondine*, the role she created in 1843 at Her Majesty's Theatre, London. (*Mary Evans Picture Library*)

RIGHT A contemporary *Giselle* danced by Makarova with the Kirov Ballet from Leningrad. (*Mike Davis Studios, Jesse Davis*)

BELOW *Ondine* was choreographed by Sir Frederick Ashton for the Royal Ballet in 1958 with Margot Fonteyn and Michael Somes dancing the leading roles. The shadow dance from this ballet became one of Fonteyn's favourite solos. (*Mike Davis Studios, Jesse Davis*)

Giselle was an instant success and was soon seen all over Europe. By 1846 it was being performed in Boston, U.S.A. and in 1860 it reached Australia. In Paris it was performed no less than 465 times, and was not dropped from the repertoire till 1868, by which time it had gone out of fashion and been largely forgotten. It has lived on because Marius Petipa kept it in the St. Petersburg repertoire and, as a result, most modern versions are in the Russian

partly because its climax was a breath-taking leap when the ballerina, escaping from the dream world to return to her lover, leapt from a six-foot-high platform into the arms of her partner – a feat that did not always come off. The story goes that one sensation-loving Englishman never missed a performance of *La Péri* because he was convinced that Grisi would kill herself one day. He was, in fact, doomed to disappointment for she lived to be 80!

La Péri had its premiere in Paris in 1843. This Drury Lane production shows the climax of the ballet when Carlotta Grisi, as the Péri queen, makes the dangerous six-foot leap into the arms of her lover. (*Mary Evans Picture Library*)

style. It is now established as one of the great ballet classics, offering the same challenge to a dancer that Hamlet offers to an actor.

Grisi herself went on to dance the role in London where she was partnered by Perrot, who had been engaged as ballet master of Her Majesty's Theatre. But though they danced together, they had ceased to sleep together, and soon afterwards she left him, reverted to her maiden name and went on to triumph on the European touring circuit.

In Paris the devoted Gautier wrote another ballet for her, *La Péri*. This was an oriental fantasy with a complicated plot built round an opium-smoking Sultan who, during his dreams, was carried away to her heavenly kingdom by a fairy queen. This ballet also became very popular,

At this time Her Majesty's Theatre (the old King's Theatre renamed after Queen Victoria's coronation in 1836) had become an important centre for ballet. Under its clever manager Benjamin Lumley, ballet reached the peak of its popularity in London during the 1840s. Like Dr. Véron in Paris before him Lumley had flair, skill and showmanship and managed to attract the best talent of the day. In his new ballet master he had a brilliant choreographer. Jules Perrot was now at the height of his powers and produced a string of memorable ballets.

One of the first was *Ondine* in 1843. This romantic story of the love of a water nymph for a human had been used for ballets before. Perrot's

Lucile Grahn is seen here in *La Fille du Bandit*, a role she created in 1846. This Danish-born dancer was trained by Bournonville in the Royal Ballet of Copenhagen and went on to international success in the capitals of Europe and in St. Petersburg. (*London, Victoria and Albert Museum*)

version became famous for its solo, the *pas de l'ombre* or shadow dance, in which Ondine sees her shadow for the first time. The leading role, which became one of Margot Fonteyn's favourites, was created by the Italian ballerina Fanny Cerrito. Trained by Carlo Blasis in Milan, this young dancer combined suppleness and strength with speed and attack as well as projecting a strong feminine appeal. She became a great favourite with English audiences and did several seasons at Her Majesty's.

ABOVE Carlotta Grisi and Jules Perrot dancing together in *La Esmeralda*. Based on Victor Hugo's novel *The Hunchback of Notre Dame*, the ballet had its premiere at Her Majesty's Theatre, London, 1844. (*Mary Evans Picture Library*)

RIGHT Ballet history was made in 1845 at Her Majesty's Theatre, London when the four leading romantic ballerinas of the day danced together in a *Pas de Quatre*, a special *divertissement* created by Perrot for a royal performance. Here are Marie Taglioni, Fanny Cerrito, Carlotta Grisi and Lucile Grahn. (*Mander & Mitchenson, Theatre Collection*)

It was Lumley's policy to engage more than one star ballerina for his theatre each season. So, the same year that Cerrito was dancing *Ondine*, Fanny Elssler was appearing in her first *Giselle*. It was Queen Victoria's idea that the two ballerinas should dance together at a command performance. Perrot arranged a special *divertissement* for them and the *Pas de Deux* by Fanny Elssler and Fanny Cerrito was the sensation of the season, which gave Lumley the idea of repeating the successful formula.

The following year Grisi returned to join the stars at Her Majesty's and to create the role of the gipsy girl in Perrot's latest ballet *La Esmeralda*. Based on Victor Hugo's best-selling novel *The Hunchback of Notre Dame*, it was one of his most important works. In London it was an immediate success, but in St. Petersburg it was an overwhelming triumph with Elssler in the leading role that was tailor-made for her temperament and talents, and that she made very much her own by bringing her pet goat onto the stage with her.

For his 1845 season Lumley had no fewer than four star ballerinas in his theatre: Taglioni, Cerrito, Grisi and a brilliant young Danish dancer Lucile Grahn. Greatly daring, Lumley decided that the four of them should dance together in an all-star *divertissement* for the queen. Jules Perrot created for them what was perhaps his finest achievement, the *Pas de Quatre*. This was pure dancing with no story. Perrot's genius lay in his understanding of each dancer and his ability to create for each one variations exactly fitted to her personality and talent.

However, handling four temperamental ballerinas was like walking through a minefield and the whole project was nearly blown up on the very day of the performance when a violent quarrel broke out about the order in which they should appear. Perrot, tearing his hair, fled to the manager's office; fortunately Lumley remained calm and, exercising the wisdom of Solomon, provided the answer. Perrot returned to the scene of battle bearing the message: 'Let the oldest dance last'. An embarrassed silence descended and peace was rapidly restored. That night the audience saw dancing that has passed into legend. In the *Pas de Quatre* four of the greatest ballerinas of the day reached the pinnacle of the romantic ballet.

This high spot also marked the beginning of its decline. The following year Marie Taglioni gave her farewell performance at Her Majesty's in Perrot's *Judgement of Paris*. The brief flowering of the romantic movement was over, but so powerful had been its impact that even today the words 'classical ballet' evoke the picture of the white ballerina in most people's minds.

Romantic ballet had, however, contained within itself the seeds of its own decadence. In Paris the cult of promoting the ballerina to the exclusion of the male dancer and the resulting prejudice against him led to the weakening of creativity and an effete type of entertainment in which women frequently danced men's roles – *ballets en travestie*.

In London the popularity of ballet declined rapidly after 1847 when the 'Swedish Nightingale' Jenny Lind arrived and started a new vogue for opera. As London had no established company or school, ballet only survived in an attenuated, popular form among the variety acts of the two great musical hall theatres, the Alhambra and the Empire, Leicester Square.

There was a sad little postscript to the romantic ballet in France in the story of Emma Livry. She made her début in 1858 in *La Sylphide* and so great was the success of this 16-year-old, that the echoes reached Taglioni in retirement by Lake Como in Italy. She came hurrying to Paris to see this young unknown in the famous role she herself had created and was so deeply impressed, recognizing in Livry her own talents and style of dancing, that she decided to stay on in Paris and train the young dancer herself. Turning choreographer she created special dances for her in a new ballet *Le Papillon* (The Butterfly) with an enchanting score by Offenbach. Its premiere in November 1860 was a triumph and Emma Livry had the world at her feet. Another ballet was planned, but it was during rehearsals that tragedy struck. As she moved forward to make an entrance, her skirt brushed against one of the naked flames of the gas jets and within seconds her whole body was engulfed in flames. Screaming, she rushed onto the stage, a human torch. A fireman managed to catch her and smother the flames but the damage was done; she was terribly burned and lived on in an agony of suffering for another eight months, dying on a summer night in 1863. She was only 21 years old. The devoted Gautier, who was at her funeral, recorded that two white butterflies hovered over her coffin as it was laid to rest in the famous cemetery in Montmartre.

Emma Livry was the last of the romantic ballerinas. Paris, shocked and grieving, had no one to follow her. But by now the centre of the ballet scene had shifted from France to Russia and the spotlight was focussed on St. Petersburg.

3

St. Petersburg

The year was 1734 and in Paris a young French dancer Jean-Baptiste Landé was packing his boxes and setting out on a slow, hazardous journey of some 2414 kilometres (1,500 miles) to take up his new post at St. Petersburg, where Anna Ivanova, Empress of Russia, had engaged him as her dancing master.

Anna, daughter of Peter the Great, was following her father's lead in turning Russia towards Western culture. Social dancing in the French style had already become part of court life and, by this time, the European idea of theatre dancing had also taken root. The Empress asked her new dancing master to arrange some *divertissements* for a court entertainment. Landé did this so successfully that Anna had the further idea of using him to train some of the children of her palace servants as dancers and this is how, in 1738, the first Russian ballet school was opened. As these were still the days of serfdom, the dancers remained the property of the Empress and so the first permanent company was formed.

Before long, dancers trained by Landé were appearing regularly in entertainments in the royal palaces in St. Petersburg and, 805 kilometres (500 miles) away, in Moscow. Landé worked on until he died in 1746, after which time an Italian impressario staged the royal entertainments. It was the new Empress Elizabeth, who was inspired to engage one of the leading ballet masters of the day, the Austrian Franz Hilverding. He arrived from Vienna bringing a troupe of his own dancers to augment the local talent. He also brought the newest ideas on the development of the dance. When he was forced to give up through ill-health, his pupil Angiolini succeeded him.

By this time, Catherine the Great was Empress of Russia and under her the arts flourished. In Moscow an embryonic ballet school started in 1773, when an enterprising dancer began training the inmates of an orphanage. From this grew the first Moscow

company, providing dancers for the new Petrovsky Theatre, later to be rebuilt and renamed the Bolshoi. St. Petersburg also had its own Bolshoi Theatre. The Maryinsky was not built until much later.

These two theatres existed for the pleasure of the Tsars and Empresses of Russia who paid lavishly for their entertainment. Opera companies as well as ballet were maintained. By the end of the century, three evenings a week were being devoted to ballet and the season usually lasted from October until the first day of Lent, in February or March.

The Director of the Imperial Theatres, responsible for arranging the programmes, was a personal appointment by the Court and he was always a Russian. Ballet masters, however, still came from Europe.

Through all the years of Catherine's reign, ballet masters from France and Italy kept Russian audiences in the mainstream of the ballet world, staging works by the leading choreographers of the day. With the new century there arrived a new ballet master whose appointment was one of the most important that had yet been made. His name was Charles Didelot and he was to lay the foundations of the Russian ballet's rise to greatness.

Born in Stockholm where his father was a leading dancer, Didelot had trained in the Swedish royal school and gone on to France to study under three of the finest teachers of the day: Noverre, Dauberval and Vestris. A fine dancer himself, he had also made his mark as a choreographer and an innovator. In London, at the King's Theatre, he had produced his best known work *Flore et Zéphire* in which he introduced 'flying ballet' on wires. He also carried the liberation of female dancers forward by introducing flesh-coloured tights. Didelot's most valuable work for Russia, however, was the series of reforms he carried out in the Imperial schools. In nine years he re-organized the whole system of teaching and gave his pupils the best French training in the Vestris tradition.

The Petipa classic ballet *La Bayadère* was first produced in 1877 and is still in the repertoire of the Kirov Ballet. Seen here is the white Act III, which is frequently performed on its own. (*Mike Davis Studios, Jesse Davis*)

His successor at St. Petersburg was another Frenchman Antoine Titus, who had been ballet master at the Berlin Court Opera. He staged the first production of *La Sylphide* in 1837 and three years later he brought to Russia the great Taglioni herself, partnered by a fine young Swedish dancer Christian Johansson.

Taglioni's success was the start of a five-year love affair with her Russian audiences, for she returned each season to delight them, while Johansson was so greatly admired that he was appointed *premier danseur* in 1841. He stayed on to devote the rest of his life to Russian ballet, becoming one of their greatest teachers.

Although foreign guest artists had so far dominated the scene, Russian dancers were by this time beginning to make their presence felt. It was a home-grown ballerina Yelena Andreyanova, who became Russia's first Giselle in 1842. She was also the first Russian ballerina to dance abroad, appearing as a guest artist in Paris and Milan.

So it came about that ballet, transplanted from France and Italy, firmly rooted itself in Russian soil. As a nation the Russians were born dancers with a long tradition of vigorous peasant folk dancing some of which can still be seen today in the Cossack style. To this strong, acrobatic dancing the French had brought grace and precision, the Italians speed and dexterity, making a superb blend of rich talent. The scene was now set for the entrance of the greatest ballet master of the century – Marius Petipa.

His entrance was not spectacular. He simply appeared quietly on the stage as a new leading dancer, engaged on a one-year contract for the 1847 season. He was then 29 years old and his career so far had not been especially distinguished. Son of a French dancer Jean Petipa, who was working as a ballet master in Marseilles, Marius and his elder brother Lucien had been trained by their father and they travelled as a family group. Marius had made his début in Brussels and gone on to dance in various provincial French towns. The family tried a tour in America but it ended in disaster and they came scuttling back to Europe. Lucien, who was the better dancer of the two brothers, went on to Paris to find fame and fortune while Marius and his father went to Spain. They were in Madrid when the note arrived from the Director of the Imperial Theatres that was to change the lives of both for, owing no doubt to some string-pulling by Marius, Petipa senior was appointed teacher in the Imperial Academy in 1848 and St. Petersburg became his home until he died in 1855.

Marius meanwhile continued his career as a dancer, often partnering the lively Fanny Elssler. His first opportunity for choreography came in 1850 when *Giselle* was revived and he was asked to make some changes in the Wilis scene. He did this so successfully that he became unofficial assistant to the new ballet master Jules Perrot and later to his successor, another Frenchman, Arthur Saint-Léon, who gave him his first chance to produce a full-length ballet.

Marius made the most of it. In 1862 he staged *La Fille du Pharaon*, a full-scale romantic ballet set in Egypt. Inspired by a work by Gautier and with music by the official composer Pugni, it was conceived on the grand scale. The original production had a cast of four hundred dancers and lasted over four hours, but it was exactly the sort of thing that audiences liked. In fact it was so successful at its premiere that Marius was immediately appointed assistant ballet master; only one more step remained. However, another seven years were to go by before Saint-Léon left to return to Paris, leaving only one of his works in the Russian repertoire, the ballet *The Little Humpbacked Horse* that had been a success, and remained popular because it was the first ballet to be based on Russian folklore. Saint-Léon left St. Petersburg in 1869. Though he had spent ten years there he had not severed his links with Paris, and he used to return regularly in the summer months when the theatres were closed. It was to Paris he returned now, with an idea for a new ballet that was to become one of the great classics: *Coppélia*.

In St. Petersburg Marius Petipa at last achieved his ambition: he was appointed ballet master in 1869. He was now 51 years old and starting on the greatest period of his life. Once again, however, it was not a spectacular start. Petipa's policy was to please his masters and, having watched Jules Perrot at loggerheads with the management, he opted for the quiet life. His first productions were

on conventional lines, suited to the mood of the time, for the Imperial taste was conservative. The Tsar and his court liked lavish spectacle, preferably in an exotic setting, and the Imperial purse paid generously for huge sets and elaborate costumes. A high standard of technical achievement was demanded as well as a story that had romantic appeal.

This difficult theatrical mix needed a choreographer of exceptional ability. In Petipa the Russians found just this for he was a superb planner. He had the organizing skill to handle huge crowds scenes; his inventive mind seemed able to work out endless variations of geometric figures for the corps de ballet, and he could also create brilliant solos and *divertissements* for the leading dancers. More than this, he had a sure instinct for public taste which he proved his first year as ballet master when, in Moscow, he produced a full-length work *Don Quixote*.

Ballet there had already begun to develop a character of its own. Moscow was a centre of commerce and theatre audiences were drawn from a much wider cross-section of people than in the court-dominated St. Petersburg. Dancing in Moscow was less polished and more robust, audiences preferred action and broad comedy, and these Petipa shrewdly provided in his version of *Don Quixote* that scored an immediate success. When, two years later, he produced the same ballet for St. Petersburg, it was in a totally different style with new choreography tuned to the tastes of a sophisticated international audience.

He followed this with a second mammoth spectacle *Bayaderka (La Bayadère)*, planned on the same successful formula as *La Fille du Pharaon*. Its premiere in St. Petersburg in February 1877 launched another classic in to the world.

This time the exotic setting is India and the romantic story is of the love of the Temple Dancer Nikia, 'La Bayadère', and Solor the young warrior who wants to marry her and swears eternal faithfulness on the sacred fire before the Temple. But Solor breaks his vow and becomes betrothed to the Princess Gamzatti daughter of the powerful Raja. Gamzatti's faithful maid Aiya rids her mistress of her rival by presenting Nikia with a basket of flowers containing a poisonous snake. Nikia is bitten and dies. A heart-broken Solor dreams of meeting her in the Kingdom of the Shades and in the third act they dance together with the ghostly spirits of the other dead *bayadères*.

It is this 'white' act that has found its way into

The Maryinsky Theatre, St. Petersburg, now renamed the Kirov Theatre, Leningrad, opened in 1866. The glamorous blue and gold interior of this famous theatre has remained almost unchanged since the days when the Tsars of Russia occupied the Imperial box seen in the centre. (*Mike Davis Studios, Jesse Davis*)

the repertoire of western companies. The complete ballet was seen by a western audience for the first time only in July 1979, when it was shown on British television direct from the Maryinsky Theatre, with the Kirov company dancing on the same stage on which the ballet had had its premiere a century before.

The blue and gold Maryinsky, now the Kirov, is one of the most glamorous theatres in the world. Its architect was an Italian Alberto Cavos, whose grandson was to pass into ballet history as a great scenic designer and founder member of Diaghilev's Ballets Russes. His name was Alexander Benois.

Built originally for the opera company and opened in 1866, the Maryinsky was not used regularly for ballet until 1889; this remained in its old home the Bolshoi Theatre of St. Petersburg. In the meantime, however, a new Director of the Imperial Theatres had been appointed who was to be the presiding genius over the fortunes of the ballet.

Ivan Vsevolojsky, a cultured, intelligent man, diplomat and artist, brought a breath of new life into the stale atmosphere of the post-romantic era and, quite suddenly in the 1880s, the popularity of the ballet began to gather momentum again in Russia. It was sparked off by the arrival of an Italian ballerina Virginia Zucchi from Milan. At this time the famous school of La Scala, Milan was turning out the most brilliant dancers of the day. Italy, which had remained more or less unaffected by the romantic movement, had gone on developing pure dance technique, displayed in huge pageant-like productions at La Scala.

Zucchi was not only a fine dancer but an actress of rare power. When she first appeared in Russia, dancing in one of the pleasure gardens of St. Petersburg, she caused such a stir that Vsevolojsky promptly engaged her for the Imperial Theatre for the 1885–6 season. It is said that when she made her début in *La Fille du Pharaon* box office receipts doubled!

The rage for ballet was on and so was the invasion of Italian ballerinas who set their audiences gasping. In Russia, as in Europe, it was the ballerina who dominated the stage. Though the sturdy, virile Russians never descended to the practice of *ballets en travestie* with women dancing men's roles, the male dancer was used mostly as a supporting partner to lift and show off the ballerina. But this was soon to change, for a male dancer arrived from Italy whose brilliant talents as a performer and as a teacher were to transform the situation. His name was Enrico Cecchetti.

Like Zucchi he made his début in one of the popular theatres in St. Petersburg in 1887, where he was soon discovered and signed up for the Imperial Theatre.

Cecchetti's dancing pedigree was impeccable. Both his parents were dancers and he had been trained in Florence by Lepri, who had himself been a pupil of the great Carlo Blasis, so the pure classical training had been passed on. Cecchetti had made his début at La Scala and gone on from there to tour the European capitals. By the time he reached Russia he had matured into a dazzling virtuoso dancer and an accomplished mime which were exactly the talents needed in an important new ballet that was being prepared.

This was to be a new venture in music. Vsevolojsky, greatly daring, had suppressed the post of official composer held by such men as Minkus and Pugni, who simply turned out melodies easy on the ear. Vsevolojsky wanted great music to go with great dancing and for the new work he had commissioned one of the leading composers of the day Pyotr Tchaikovsky to write the score for a ballet entitled *The Sleeping Beauty*.

It was a risky decision. Tchaikovsky had only written one ballet score previously and that had been a failure when presented in Moscow twelve years before. It was called *Swan Lake*!

Tchaikovsky, deciding that ballet music was not his line, had never tried again. Now he was being asked to work in a medium for which he thought he was not suited, collaborating with an aged, dictatorial ballet master who was accustomed to ordering his music by the bar.

Such a situation would seem to be asking for trouble: a 72-year-old choreographer accustomed to having his own way, and a 50-year-old composer whose only discipline had been that of his own genius. Surely it must end in a violent clash of temperaments, or else the shopping list of so many bars of three-four waltz time and so on would kill the composer's inspiration. Astonishingly the reverse happened. Tchaikovsky seemed to find the rigid discipline imposed on him a challenge and a stimulus to his creative ideas. The great music of *The Sleeping Beauty* poured out in a sparkling stream as though it were completely spontaneous.

The ballet went into rehearsal with an Italian dancer in the leading role. Carlotta Brianza, *prima*

Virginia Zucchi, the Italian-born dancer trained by Blasis in Milan, was one of the first Italian ballerinas to appear in St. Petersburg, where her brilliant virtuoso technique and strong dramatic impact triggered off a tremendous revival of enthusiasm for ballet. This picture of her was taken about 1885. (*Collection of Natalia Roslavleva; Novosti Press Agency*)

Swan Lake today. Turned into a trimphant success by
Petipa in 1895, Tchaikovsky's 'failure' is seen here danced
by the Bolshoi Ballet, with Bessmertnova and Lavrovsky in
the leading roles. (*Mike Davis Studios, Jesse Davis*)

BELOW A rare glimpse of the first, unsuccessful production of
Swan Lake at the Bolshoi Theatre, Moscow in 1877, with
choreography by Reisinger and costumes and settings by a

group of five Russian artists. (*Mander & Mitchenson Theatre
Collection*)

OPPOSITE Many dancers have become specially identified
with certain roles in *The Sleeping Beauty*. This is true of Maria
Petipa the original Lilac Fairy, and also of South African-
born Deanne Bergsma, who was charming in the part. (*Mike
Davis Studios, Jesse Davis*)

ballerina of La Scala and a dancer of sensational
technique, was to be partnered by the fine Russian
dancer Pavel Gerdt. Petipa's daughter Maria was
to create the role of the Lilac Fairy, while the
newcomer Enrico Cecchetti was given two contrasting roles. As the wicked fairy Carabosse he had
full scope for his talent in mime, and as the Blue
Bird in the *pas de deux* at Aurora's wedding he could
display his virtuosity. The speed and precision of
his *entrechats* and pirouettes were sensational and
with such material to work on Petipa's choreography reached a new height of brilliance. The
Bluebird *pas de deux* is still an exacting test for any
dancer today.

The story of *The Sleeping Beauty* followed the
well-known fairy tale by Charles Perrault. As he
had lived in the time of Louis XIV, the sets were in
the grand Versailles manner. No fewer than six
scenic designers worked on these huge sets, while
Vsevolojsky himself designed many of the costumes.
History was made on 16 January 1890 in the
Maryinksy Theatre when the fabulously expensive

Sleeping Beauty had its premiere in the presence of the Tsar. The first night audience awarded it a triumphant reception and the ballet went on to become one of the world's great classics.

St. Petersburg was now riding on the crest of the wave. Two years later another great classic was launched, *The Nutcracker* with Tchaikovsky's music

Maria Petipa, daughter of the great Marius Petipa, architect of classical Russian ballet, is seen here in her costume for the Polish Mazurka in *Diable à Quatre* at the Paris Opéra in 1882. She was later to create the role of the Lilac Fairy in her father's ballet *The Sleeping Beauty*. (*Mander & Mitchenson Theatre Collection*)

to Petipa's libretto taken from a story by Hoffmann. This time, however, Petipa was not able to see his production through for he fell ill and had to hand over the choreography to his assistant Ivanov. Here was a Russian-trained dancer who never managed to come to the top. It seems likely that his personality did not match his gifts and that he lacked the drive and ability to assert himself, so he

ABOVE LEFT Born in Italy and trained at La Scala, Milan, Pierina Legnani made ballet history in St. Petersburg in 1893 when she appeared in the premiere of *Cinderella*, and the Maryinsky audience saw for the first time her famous thirty-two *fouettés*. (*London, Victoria and Albert Museum*)

ABOVE RIGHT Christian Johansson the Swedish-born dancer, was trained by the Danish Bournonville in the pure French tradition of Auguste Vestris, before coming to St. Petersburg in 1841 as a leading dancer. He achieved immediate success and remained there for the rest of his life, first as a dancer and then as a brilliant teacher in the Imperial school, where he laid the foundation of the superb Russian style of dancing. (*Collection of Natalia Roslavleva; Novosti Press Agency*)

BELOW Nicolas Legat, born in St. Petersburg in 1869 and Olga Preobrajenska, born in St. Petersburg in 1870 are two of the generation of brilliant Russian dancers to emerge from the Imperial schools in the 1880s and '90s. They both appeared in the premiere of *The Nutcracker* in 1892, and were later to bring their superb technique to the young dancers of Europe when Legat opened his school in London and Preobrajenska hers in Paris. They are seen here dancing together in two *Pas de Deux*. (*Mander & Mitchenson Theatre Collection*)

lived under the shadow of the dominating Petipa and his work never received the recognition it deserved during his lifetime. It is only with the passing of the years that its true value has come to be realized.

The Nutcracker is the doll given to the child Clara (also Marie or Masha) by her godfather Drosselmayer at a Christmas party. When she falls asleep the Nutcracker comes to life and leads an army of toy soldiers into battle against an invasion of mice. It then turns into a handsome prince who takes her to the Kingdom of Sweets where the Sugar Plum Fairy honours them with a grand *divertissement*. This is an occasion for a brilliant display of individual talent. *The Nutcracker* has become one of the most frequently danced ballets in the world, passing through the hands of many choreographers until only one fragment remains of the original by Ivanov – the grand *pas de deux* of the Sugar Plum Fairy and her cavalier.

Sadly, this ballet was the last of the astonishing Petipa-Tchaikovsky partnership. Plans were made for a third work *Cinderella*, but Petipa fell ill again and Tchaikovsky died of cholera. *Cinderella* was, however, produced with choreography by Ivanov and Cecchetti to music by Boris Schell. Like *Sleeping Beauty*, Perrault's tale is a gift to ballet. *Cinderella* has been recreated and rescored by dance companies all over the world and still remains a box office favourite. The Maryinsky production had its

premiere in December 1893. The leading role was taken by a new Italian Ballerina Pierina Legnani, who had been appearing in London's new Alhambra Theatre earlier in the year, where she had astounded her audiences by a feat of technique that had never been seen before. Now the Russians were to witness it.

In one of her solos she started on a classical *fouetté* which is the quick whipping movement of one leg from the knee as the dancer circles. There was nothing new about this except that Legnani did not stop. The audience stared, opera glasses were riveted on the whirling figure. They were counting now and could hardly believe it as she reached a breath-taking thirty-two *fouettés*.

Legnani was a sensation as well as the envy of the other dancers. One of those watching her was a brilliant performer herself, Mathilda Kschessinska, who had graduated only three years before and had already been promoted *prima ballerina*. Determined to match Legnani's brilliance, she went back to the practice studio to master the secret and in due course she became the first Russian dancer to achieve it. She was also the first Russian Princess Aurora in *The Sleeping Beauty*.

In the meantime Legnani became a regular visitor to St. Petersburg and was to make ballet history yet again when she created the role of Odette–Odile in the immortal *Swan Lake* in 1895.

The story of this four-act ballet is based on a German folk tale. The Princess Odette and her maidens have been turned into swans by the magician Rotbart and only regain their human form for a few hours at midnight. It is on one such occasion that Prince Siegfried meets Odette, falls in love, and swears to rescue her by choosing her as his bride at a ball in the castle. Siegfried, however, is tricked by Rotbart who brings his daughter Odile, the black swan, looking exactly like Odette to the ball. As Siegfried makes his fatal promise a terrible storm erupts and everything is plunged into darkness. Siegfried, realizing he has been deceived, rushes out to find his true love. They are reunited by the lakeside, Odette forgives him, and they finally escape the magician's power by plunging into the lake to be together in eternity. This, at least, is one of the more usual endings. Some

The second ballet by Tchaikovsky, Petipa and Ivanov, *The Nutcracker*, had its premiere at the Maryinsky Theatre in December 1892 and has become one of the world's great classics. It is danced here by the Bolshoi Ballet with Maximova as Clara and Vasiliev as the Nutcracker. (*Mike Davis Studios, Jesse Davis*)

47

The young Pavlova: born in St. Petersburg in 1881, she died in the Hague in 1931. Anna Pavlova travelled the world with missionary zeal to bring her art to people in every country. She inspired countless youngsters to train for ballet, and her name still stands as a symbol of the immoral figure of the great classical ballerina. (*Mander & Mitchenson Theatre Collection*)

premiere in January 1895 when, once again, Legnani and her famous thirty-two *fouettés* scored a triumph. She left her mark permanently on the ballet, for this feat is still regularly performed in many present-day productions.

By this time, however, the supremacy of the Italian ballerinas was over and a brilliant new generation of Russian-trained dancers was emerging who could more than match their rivals. This was the result of years of patient work in the ballet school by their chief teacher Christian Johansson. For nearly thirty years he devoted himself to the task of passing on to his pupils the pure classical teaching he had learned from Bournonville, and it was he, more than anyone, who built up the superb style that is the hallmark of the Russian school of dancing.

Thanks to Johansson, and to the influence of Cecchetti who was also teaching in the school by this time, the male dancer was coming back into his own. The 1880s and '90s saw the graduation of young men who were to become great names: Serge Legat and his brother Nicolas, who was to step into Petipa's shoes; Alexander Gorsky and Mikhail Mordkin, who were to make ballet history in Moscow and Mikhail Fokine, choreographer of genius, who was to bring Russian ballet back to Europe with Diaghilev. With them came the great Russian ballerinas and teachers of the future: Preobrajenska, Egorova, Trefilova who were to take great dancing across the world and, in 1889, the 18-year-old Anna Pavlova, the unique, solitary figure of the immortal ballerina.

For Petipa and Johansson this was the climax of their long years of work. They were both old men now, nearing the end of their lives, and the curtain was about to go up on a new and very different scene.

As the three dominant figures of the nineteenth-century ballet, Petipa, Johansson and Tchaikovsky, faded into the shadows, three young men were waiting in the wings to make their entry with the new century. Their names were Diaghilev, Fokine and Stravinsky and with them modern ballet arrived.

versions have altered it to a satisfying destruction of the wicked magician and the freeing of the swan maidens.

Petipa, now an astonishing 77 years old, created the choreography for Acts I and III himself, that is, the castle and ballroom scenes. The white Acts II and IV he entrusted to Ivanov who produced some inspired choreography which still keeps its freshness and lyrical beauty. The ballet had its

4

Pre-War Diaghilev

On the threshold of the twentieth century two events took place in St. Petersburg which, at the time, were of only local interest, but in the story of ballet can be seen as the first ripples of the new tidal wave that was building up to surge across Europe.

In 1898 a 19-year-old dancer graduated from the Imperial Academy. He had shown such brilliance that he by-passed the usual *corps de ballet* appointment and stepped straight into the rank of soloist; his name was Mikhail Fokine. The same year a new magazine appeared, *The World of Art*. This was a controversial, forward-looking publication presenting the ideas of the younger generation and its editor was a young man of 26 called Serge Diaghilev.

The St. Petersburg of those days was a ferment of new ideas. The smell of rebellion was in the air, and this was not only political, for the arts, sensitive as always to every current of feeling, were pointing the way. Spearheaded by the young artist Alexander Benois, the musician Walter Nouvel and their circle of friends, the new generation were pushing against the restricting walls of old tradition.

'Art for art's sake' was the cry and Diaghilev was in the thick of the battle. Though he was neither an artist nor a musician himself, he was very much a leader – a powerful personality who knew how to make his presence felt. He was also a highly cultured man. Brought up in the heart of Russia he had been steeped in music; all his family were musical and it was commonplace for them to organize concerts or produce whole operas for their own pleasure or to entertain their friends. So, knowledge of music and a habit of autocratic authority were bred into young Serge. His interest in art had come later, aroused by his friendship with Benois and another artist Léon Bakst, whom Diaghilev first met when he came to St. Petersburg as a university student – ostensibly to study law!

His new friends failed, however, to interest him in ballet. They themselves were great Maryinsky enthusiasts but young Serge preferred opera and concerts. Then, as *The World of Art* got under way he took up the idea of holding art exhibitions and discovered in himself his organizing ability and his

Serge Diaghilev photographed in Monte Carlo, which was to become the home and headquarters of his Ballets Russes. (*Mander & Mitchenson Theatre Collection*)

Isadora Duncan believed passionately in freedom of movement and self-expression. Discarding all the conventions of classical ballet, she always appeared on stage bare-foot, in flowing Greek-style draperies. Her ideas were a powerful influence in Europe where she started the trend towards modern dancing. (*Mary Evans Picture Library*)

flair for publicity. He also developed his talent for finding financial backing.

Diaghilev had an extraordinary capacity for making friends and this was to be one of the keys to his success. It was not a case of merely touching people for cash, he was able to arouse their enthusiasm and draw them into the orbit of his creative ventures. One of his earliest personal triumphs was the friendship and powerful backing of the Grand Duke Vladimir Alexandrovitch, a cousin of the Tsar. He helped Diaghilev launch his first exhibition of Russian art in Paris. From this success followed the idea of taking Russian music to Paris and in 1907 the Grand Duke backed a successful concert season, followed by a season of Russian opera during which Diaghilev brought to Paris the great bass singer Chaliapin. From here it was only a step to the idea of bringing Russian dancers to Paris.

In the meantime, the dancers themselves, though hidden behind the protective walls of the Imperial Academy, were also feeling the current of new ideas surging through their city.

Young Fokine had been discovering his talent for choreography. His first ballet *Acis and Galatea*, based on a pastoral theme and created for a senior pupils' annual display, had shown such marked originality and poetic quality that he had gone on to do the choreography for charity performances.

For one of these occasions he created a solo for his fellow student and partner Anna Pavlova. Although it was put together in only a few minutes, Fokine created a deeply moving dance of great lyrical beauty that is forever linked with her name – *The Dying Swan*. In Pavlova he found a perfect interpreter of his ideas and for her he also created a romantic white-tutu waltz that formed part of a series of dances he had arranged to the music of Chopin. First seen at a charity show in 1907 under the title *Chopiniana*, it was later given to the world by Diaghilev as *Les Sylphides*.

At this time also, the world of Russian ballet, that now seemed so set in its ways, received a severe jolt. Isadora Duncan arrived in St. Petersburg waving the banner of freedom for the dance.

This remarkable young American believed passionately that a dancer should be free to express her feelings through movement. She rebelled against the artificial constrictions of tutus, tights and blocked shoes, and against the convention of stylized ballet movements. She appeared on stage bare-foot, in filmy, Greek-style draperies, dancing to the music of great composers like Beethoven and

Schubert. She danced with a passionate intensity of feeling and such was the magnetic power of her personality that she carried her audience with her. Diaghilev saw her and was enthusiastic; Pavlova saw her and was genuinely admiring; Fokine saw her and, though he was not converted, he received a powerful stimulus to his own creative development. These strands were all to come together in the Diaghilev plan to bring Russian ballet to Paris in 1909.

Actually a more compelling personal reason had stimulated Diaghilev's sudden interest in ballet. He had not long before met a young Maryinsky dancer Vaslav Nijinsky and fallen deeply in love.

It was Diaghilev's private tragedy that he was only attracted to virile young men who, in the nature of things, were likely to abandon him. Nijinsky at 20 years old was a superb specimen of muscular young male. He had graduated from the

Pavlova in *The Dying Swan*, the solo created for her by fellow student Fokine in St. Petersburg in 1907, which became her hallmark, and which she continued to dance for the rest of her life. This painting by Ernst Oppler appeared in *L'Illustration* in 1928. (*Mary Evans Picture Library*)

Imperial school only the year before but behind him lay nine years of highly disciplined training which had developed him into a magnificent dancer with a powerful stage presence. On stage Nijinsky was a god; off stage he was a stocky little man only 1.7 metres (5ft 4in) tall, with slavonic features and a withdrawn expression. Most people found him completely inarticulate. The unkind said that he was dim-witted and that this was proved by the fact that he failed his written graduation examinations the first time, and would probably have failed the second time also if he had not been such a brilliant dancer. His friends, however, loyally maintained that he had hidden depths of creative ability that he could not express in words, but only through movement, and that his withdrawn attitude was a protective defence that he had developed as a result of being bullied as a child.

Certainly when he met Diaghilev he was still immature. The sheltered life of the Imperial school tended to hold back slow developers. He was not, however, a wide-eyed innocent as has been suggested for he had already been led along the homosexual path by one of the Russian princes,

who had taken him up almost as soon as he made his first stage appearance and lavished favours on him. Then, with rare and sensitive foresight, the prince had handed him over to Diaghilev who seemed the man most able to do great things for the young dancer.

At that stage Nijinsky seemed happy enough to be treated like a parcel. All that really mattered to him was his art, and he must quickly have realized that Diaghilev was a man who could open up exciting new prospects for him in his career and take him beyond the frustrating confines of the Maryinsky. He willingly accepted Diaghilev's invitation to be part of the company he was assembling for Paris. In those days dancers were free to accept other engagements during the summer months when the Imperial theatres were closed.

Diaghilev engaged as Nijinsky's partner a charming young soloist Tamara Karsavina, who had graduated in 1902 but had not yet been promoted ballerina. He needed a star so he approached Anna Pavlova, a ballerina now of two years standing, who was already seen as one of the great dancers of the future. The male star was to be Mikhail Mordkin, leading dancer and ballet master of the Bolshoi in Moscow. Diaghilev also engaged Adolph Bolm from the Maryinsky and a strong *corps de ballet* drawn from both theatres. With Benois and Fokine he planned a wide-ranging repertoire.

Enthusiasm mounted as they went into rehearsal. Then misfortune struck. Only a few weeks before the opening, their friend and backer the Grand Duke Vladimir Alexandrovitch died. It seemed a total disaster for at one stroke they had lost a powerful patron, a great deal of money and the privileged use of the Maryinsky scenery and costumes. A lesser man might have given up but Diaghilev was a fighter. All the aggressive power that had made him so many enemies was now channelled into his determination to survive. He found new patrons and he kept his company of dancers together. The disaster was, in fact, to lead to even greater success for Benois and Bakst had to set to work to create completely new décors and costumes.

More fighting was needed over the theatre in Paris. Unable to get into the Opéra they booked the Châtelet, an old barn of a place accustomed to rough musichall audiences. This would not do at all for Diaghilev the aristocrat. He had the entire place redecorated and carpeted, sparing no expense

to make it fit for the type of audience he intended to attract, and he also had the stage relaid to make it fit for his dancers.

Posters announcing 'Les Ballets Russes' appeared in the Paris streets and a calculated whispering campaign sent the news through society's grapevine that here was something not to be missed.

The young Nijinsky, aged 19, in 1907 the year he graduated from the Imperial school, St. Petersburg after nine years training. (*Mander & Mitchenson Theatre Collection*)

On the night of 19 May 1909 the theatre was packed with a brilliant audience and the curtain went up on a season that opened a new era in the history of the ballet. French audiences were seeing for the first time the superb dancing of the Russian school. They saw Fokine's *Pavillon d'Armide* with Mordkin partnering a young dancer from the Bolshoi Vera Koralli, who was to become Russia's first film star. They saw the new version of *Chopiniana*, now *Les Sylphides*, with Pavlova, Karsavina and Nijinsky. It was a feast of beautiful

LEFT Nijinsky in *Giselle* in 1911. (*Mander & Mitchenson Theatre Collection*)

BELOW Tamara Karsavina, who died as recently as 1978, was trained in the Imperial school and was appointed ballerina of the Maryinsky Theatre in 1909. That year Diaghilev engaged her as a partner for Nijinsky in his new touring company. She is seen here in *Giselle* in 1911. (*Mander & Mitchenson Theatre Collection*)

dancing but the audience, while admiring the dancers, were already familiar with narrative ballet and the romantic white ballet. What they had never seen was powerful male dancing, so when the curtain went up on the *Polovtsian Dances* from the opera *Prince Igor* and the stage was filled with virile, acrobatic young men dancing to Borodin's exciting rhythms, the Parisians went wild.

There was more to come. The exotic ballet *Cleopatra* dazzled them with the brilliant colours of Bakst's décor and swept them away on a passionate

OPPOSITE *The Firebird* was the first of a brilliant series of ballets combining Fokine's choreography and Stravinsky's music. First produced in Paris in 1910, it is now danced by many companies; this picture shows the finale of the Royal Ballet production. (*Mike Davis Studios, Jesse Davis*)

LEFT Karsavina with Adolph Bolm in the original production of *The Firebird* in 1910. (*Mansell Collection*)

ABOVE Leon Bakst's set design for *Schéhérezade*. The ballet had a triumphant premiere in Paris in June 1910 at a time when the fashion for the exotic was at its height. (*Mansell Collection*)

tide of sensual beauty and drama. They found Nijinsky's dancing sensational and they were captivated by the beauty of Cleopatra herself, a ravishing young Jewess named Ida Rubinstein, who was perfect for the role except that she was virtually untrained as a dancer. She had, in fact, been one of Fokine's private pupils and it was his daring idea to use her. He carefully choreographed her role to disguise her weakness and relied upon the virtuosity of Karsavina and Pavlova to provide

55

Cleopatra was the first of the new exotic ballets that were to take Paris by storm. Nijinsky and Karsavina are seen here in the ballet's first production in May 1910. (*Mander & Mitchenson Theatre Collection*)

Enrico Cecchetti appearing as the Grand Eunuch in *Schéhérezade*. (*Mander & Mitchenson Theatre Collection*)

great classical dancing. The gamble paid off. Rubinstein became the toast of Paris and started a new fashion for the exotic.

The season was a triumph. Diaghilev's Ballets Russes were launched on a spectacular wave of success and with them Vaslav Nijinsky. The only people who were not happy were the stars Pavlova and Mordkin who felt they had been overshadowed by the newcomers.

For Pavlova and Diaghilev it was to be the parting of the ways. Pavlova was, above all, an individualist. Diaghilev was a team man. For her, ballet was the solo dance. For him it was a complete work of art blending dancing, music and décor. So Pavlova went on her solitary way – a great star glittering brilliantly as she travelled on her mission to bring classical ballet to the world.

Partnered first by Mordkin and supported by a small company of dancers, she took her art to the far corners of the earth. In draughty halls, on small stages in unsuitable theatres, the frail, indomitable figure of the great ballerina brought the superb art of classical ballet to thousands until she killed herself by overwork. But she fired a whole generation with the ambition to become dancers. Pavlova was to fill the ballet schools of the future, while Diaghilev filled the theatres.

A scene from the original production of *Petrushka* in Paris in 1911, with Nijinsky and Karsavina as the clown and the ballerina. (*Mander & Mitchenson Theatre Collection*)

The second Paris season of the Ballets Russes was an even greater triumph. Igor Stravinsky joined the team and out of this fusion of creative genius emerged three great new ballets.

The Firebird, based on a blend of Russian fairy tales, was danced to Stravinsky's music that brilliantly captured the authentic Russian atmosphere and delighted the Paris audiences. An even greater impact was made by the exotic successor to *Cleopatra*. The new ballet *Schéhérezade* was based on a story from *A Thousand and One Nights*. It combined the genius of Benois who wrote the book, Fokine who created the choreography to the music of Rimsky-Korsakov and a sensational setting by Bakst. *Schéhérezade* has been described as sex, savagery and sadism packaged in gorgeous colours and Parisians received this sensual shock with rapture. The impact of Nijinsky as the Gold Slave was tremendous.

In complete contrast was *Carnaval* – a light-hearted Harlequin and Columbine romp in the Italian Commedia del' arte or 'pantomime' tradition danced to the music of Schumann, again with Fokine's choreography. It introduced a delightful young dancer just out of school, Lydia Lopokova, as Columbine partnered by Nijinsky. This too captured the mood of the time and was received with delight. The only ballet that made very little impact was the classical offering *Giselle* and Diaghilev never repeated it.

He had no reason to worry, however. Two triumphant seasons in Paris had launched the Russian ballet in Europe. Diaghilev was riding high. He had Nijinsky at his side and the world at his feet, and the coming year was to see the climax of his achievement.

The year 1911 opened with performances in Rome and Monte Carlo followed by a Paris season, interrupted briefly for a first appearance in London at a special gala performance at Covent Garden in honour of King George V's coronation. The success of this led to an engagement for a London season in the autumn.

That year the new ballet was *Petrushka*, in which Fokine reached the heights of his choreographic genius and Nijinsky created what many think of as his greatest role. The ballet began life as the germ of an idea by Stravinsky. He had a sudden

The set for the BBC television production of *Petrushka* showing the old Butter Fair market in St. Petersburg. (*Mike Davis Studios, Jesse Davis*)

RIGHT *Petrushka* is danced today by companies all over the world. This is a scene from the production by the Royal Ballet. (*Mike Davis Studios, Jesse Davis*)

inspiration for a musical score that would describe a duel between a puppet, represented by the piano and the orchestra. This caught on with Benois who had long cherished the idea of a ballet that would recreate the old Shrovetide Fair in St. Petersburg, and together they developed the story of the ill-used sawdust puppet who has a soul over which his master the Magician has no control.

Petrushka is one of three puppets belonging to the Magician who displays them to the crowd. They are the black-faced Moor in a splendid uniform, the pretty, heartless Ballerina and Petrushka the sad clown. Behind the scenes the puppets have lives of their own and human emotions. Petrushka is in love with the Ballerina who flirts with him but prefers the Moor. The unhappy Petrushka, crazy with jealousy, desperately attacks his powerful rival who chases him out into the square. Before the horrified crowd the Moor kills Petrushka. The Magician is hastily summoned. He picks up the limp body to show that it is only a doll with the sawdust running out. As the crowd disperses, however, the ghost of Petrushka is seen above the puppet-booth cursing his master.

58

The ballet had its premiere in Paris on 13 June 1911. It revealed Nijinsky as an actor of intense power and many have since seen it as prophetic of his own tragic story. It has passed into the repertoires of most of the major companies and ranks as one of the great ballets of the world.

The other great ballet that season was no more than a romantic fragment yet, as with the *Dying Swan*, Fokine created a small masterpiece and *Le Spectre de la Rose* is for ever associated with the legendary partnership of Nijinsky and Karsavina.

Based on a poem by Gautier and danced to the romantic waltz strains of Weber's music, it tells the story of a young girl after her first ball. She is dreaming in her room as she holds the red rose given to her by her first lover. As she dreams the living Spirit of the Rose comes leaping through the open window. They dance together in a dream world of romantic ecstasy until the dawn brings the moment of farewell and the Rose vanishes, as he has come, with a spectacular leap through the window.

A romantic story of this type, with a man dressed in rose petals, could all too easily have sunk to the level of cheap sentimentality but such was the artistry of Karsavina and Nijinsky that they raised it to the heights of pure classical ballet. It was to pave the way for the proper appreciation of the other great classical white ballets that the French audiences had failed to understand.

Though the French had to be re-educated in their appreciation of classical ballet, the English audiences had never lost touch with the great tradition, thanks to visiting artists from the continent, and for his English audiences in the autumn of 1911 Diaghilev had two special treats in store. From the treasures of Petipa days he gave them *Swan Lake* and, from *The Sleeping Beauty*, the *pas de deux* of Aurora and her Prince. More than this, he succeeded in bringing over the great Kschessinska, *prima ballerina assoluta* of the Maryinksy.

The Ballets Russes were now at the height of their fame and Diaghilev could have sat back and made himself a rich man by simply repeating the theatre-filling successes he had already created. But this was not in his nature. He was a pioneer; he needed to go forward, to explore. He also enjoyed surprising or even shocking his audiences.

LEFT The original roles in the miniature classic *Le Spectre de la Rose* were created in 1911 by Nijinsky and Karsavina. They are danced here by Alexis Rassine and the young Margot Fonteyn. (*John Topham Picture Library*)

Le Dieu Bleu, the ballet written by Jean Cocteau, had its premiere in Paris in 1913. Karsavina is seen here dancing with Fokine, who did the choreography. (*Mander & Mitchenson Theatre Collection*)

OVERLEAF Nijinsky's second attempt at choreography was *Le Sacre du Printemps*. The artistic importance of the ballet is now recognized and several contemporary versions exist; this is a Royal Ballet production. (*Mike Davis Studios, Jesse Davis*)

The following year his audiences were not only shocked but scandalized. On 29 May 1912 at the Théâtre du Châtelet the curtain went up on *L'Après-midi d'un Faune (The Afternoon of a Faun)*, a ballet that not only launched Nijinsky as a choreographer but pointed the way Diaghilev's ballets were to develop in the future.

Le Faune is set in ancient Greece. The idea had been born when Nijinsky, Diaghilev and Bakst had gone there on a visit and had become enthusiastic about creating a ballet derived from the sculptured figures on classical Greek bas-reliefs. This was the opportunity for which Diaghilev had been waiting, to give Nijinsky his first experience of creating a new ballet. Contradictory opinions have raged about the value and originality of Nijinsky's work. One thing is certain, however, the process of creation was incredibly slow. Nijinsky shut himself away in a room for hours on end to work out his ideas. Unable to express himself in words he had physically to show the dancers what he wanted. As a result it took one hundred-and-twenty rehearsals to complete a ten minute ballet for eight dancers.

The result was a totally new type of ballet. Gone were the great elevations, the fluid lyrical movements. This was flat, angular, with sudden staccato movements. Nijinsky had broken away from the classical mimed story and was using the dance to create images that expressed emotions. The day of the expressionist ballet had arrived.

The emotions expressed in *Le Faune* are clearly sexual. A carefree young faun, on a spring afternoon, frolics with a group of nymphs. They all run away except one who returns to dance with him until she too is alarmed by the violence of his passion, breaks free and escapes. Left alone, the faun picks up the scarf she has dropped, fondles it and stretches himself out on it.

It was this final erotic act that shocked the first night Paris audience into shouts of protest. Diaghilev's reaction to the uproar was typical of the man. He had the entire ballet repeated. The next day the whole episode was reported in the papers and it triggered off a violent controversy. The result was full houses, and Diaghilev was delighted.

Unfortunately, the shock waves surrounding *Le Faune* completely eclipsed another, more important work by Fokine, *Daphnis and Chloë* and at the end of the season Fokine left the company. His departure left Diaghilev unmoved. He had Nijinsky and he was preparing yet another shock for Paris – *Le Sacre du Printemps (Rite of Spring)*.

The idea for this ballet had come from Stravinsky. Collaborating with the painter Nicholas Roerich, he evolved a story of the primitive fertility rites of ancient Russia when a beautiful young girl is offered as a human sacrifice to the goddess of spring. Stravinsky created a fine modern score

L'Après-midi d'un Faune. This erotic, modern-style ballet, choreographed by Nijinsky, caused a scandal at its premiere in Paris in 1912. This photograph from the original production shows Nijinsky as the faun. (*Mander & Mitchenson Theatre Collection*)

RIGHT Nijinsky's avant-garde choreography and Stravinsky's modern music sparked off an uproar at the premiere in Paris in 1913 of *Le Sacre du Printemps (The Rite of Spring)*. Among the dancers in the original production was the young Marie Rambert. (*Mander & Mitchenson Theatre Collection*)

evoking vast primaeval forces but for the dancers the complicated music created vast problems. These were not helped by Nijinsky's choreography which they found complex and difficult. Rehearsals became a time of mounting tension. Nijinsky, under strain, became awkward and bad tempered; Stravinsky had his patience severely tried as Nijinsky could not even read a musical score, and Diaghilev had increasingly to intervene to maintain discipline.

In the end he engaged a young dancer to help out. She was Marie Rambert, a pupil from the Jaques-Dalcroze School of Eurythmics, where she had been taught his system of movement to express rhythm in music. The talented Marie was a lively, extrovert young woman of 25. Born in Poland, the daughter of a Jewish family, she had been brought up in Warsaw where her father kept a bookshop. Her love of dancing found expression early, she

became an enthusiastic follower of Isadora Duncan and, as soon as she was old enough, Marie went to Paris as one of her disciples. This bare-foot dancing was followed by training at the Dalcroze Institute at Hellerau in East Germany. Then, as part of the *corps de ballet* in Diaghilev's company, she put on ballet shoes and received a classical training from Cecchetti, while the slow and painful rehearsals of *Le Sacre* continued all through the winter at Monte Carlo.

The premiere of *Le Sacre* was to be the main event at the opening of the smart new Théâtre de Champs-Elysées in Paris. It created an uproar. The impact of the new expressionist, abstract ideas, forcefully combined in the music, dancing and décor, produced first bewilderment and then re-vulsion. Half the audience started hissing, and the other half clapping to silence them. When it came to the sacrificial scene the smart crowd seemed to go berserk and behaved like football hooligans. The noise they made almost drowned the music. When the company moved on to London the more phlegmatic British public received *Le Sacre* with polite astonishment and there was no repetition of the Paris uproar.

This was the last of Nijinsky's ballets for Diaghilev. Already the great dream was crumbling and the intimacy of their relationship was under-going a subtle change. A few weeks later Nijinsky was to bring the whole ambitious structure that he and Diaghilev had built together crashing in ruins about them.

He got married.

The bombshell reached Diaghilev in the form of a cable from his valet in South America, where the company were on tour that autumn of 1913, for Diaghilev, who had a superstitious terror of sea journeys, had dropped out at the last minute and remained in Europe. A three-week voyage under tropical skies had sparked off a shipboard romance between Nijinsky and Romola de Pulska, a beauti-ful ash-blonde Hungarian dancer in the *corps de ballet*, and they were married in Buenos Aires soon after the company landed. Far away in Venice, Diaghilev's reaction was one of shock and anger, followed by the depression of a man deeply hurt. Nijinsky had not only been disloyal, he had not even had the courage to break the news himself. In fact another three weeks were to go by before a letter arrived from the Argentine. By this time Diaghilev the fighter was back in action and Nijinsky had been shut out of his life.

Diaghilev's immediate objective was to find a choreographer and leading dancer, and he had no scruples about turning once more to Fokine, whom he had treated so badly. It is said that it took a five-hour conversation on the telephone to persuade Fokine in Russia to rejoin the company. True or not, the blend of Diaghilev charm and pressure succeeded and Fokine agreed.

65

La Légende de Joseph, Diaghilev's last pre-war ballet, first produced in April 1914, launched a new star the 19-year-old Léonide Massine. Recently graduated from the Bolshoi school in Moscow, he created the role of Joseph, and is seen here in the original production, with the set designed by Sert and costumes by Bakst. (*Mander & Mitchenson Theatre Collection*)

When the company reassembled for the new season Nijinsky was no longer with them. He had been dismissed. Marie Rambert also found herself out of a job. She went on to Paris courageously to continue her career giving solo dance recitals. In this way she laid the foundation of her own reputation, and of the ballet company that bears her name today.

In the meantime the posters for the Ballets Russes went up outside the Paris Opéra announcing the season's repertoire. The Nijinsky ballets had vanished and the main work was a new ballet *La Légende de Joseph*. Based on the Old Testament story, with music specially written by Richard Strauss, the choreography had been taken over by Fokine. Unfortunately neither he nor the composer were at their most inspired and the ballet failed to make much impression. It did serve, however, to launch its leading dancer – a young man whom Diaghilev had discovered after a long search, in the Bolshoi Theatre – Léonide Massine.

Diaghilev was taking a great chance giving a big role to a 17-year-old, but the slender, athletic young dancer, with his clean-cut good looks and large brown eyes, exactly fitted the picture of Joseph that Diaghilev had in mind. Once again his flair and daring paid off. Massine was an instant success both in Paris and London.

By now the rumbling of threatened war was getting dangerously close. When, on 25 July, the curtain came down at Covent Garden on the last performance at the end of the season, it came down also on the end of an era. A few days later on 4 August 1914, Europe was plunged into war.

5

Post-War Diaghilev

For a European the 1914–18 war was a hell-filled black gulf that swallowed up a whole generation of young men and destroyed a whole way of life.

The bright, brittle young survivors emerging from the nightmare of death and shattered nerves, drowned the echoes of the guns with the strident discords of jazz. On the dance floors, the gracious valeta and the waltz were replaced by the frenetic foxtrot and the Charleston.

For a Russian in exile there was a double nightmare for the red tide of revolution had battered down the old autocratic power of the Tsars and set up the rule of the people under the hammer and sickle.

For Serge Diaghilev nothing could ever be the same again. He had lost everything he had built up. The brilliantly talented group that had surrounded him had scattered. Cut off from the country he loved, he was facing middle age, exile and poverty. But still Diaghilev the fighter was not beaten; he had one dancer left at his side – Léonide Massine, and he courageously set to work to rebuild his company round this young man. He also had the ageing maestro Cecchetti at hand in Italy.

In Massine he found a quick, receptive mind well able to express itself. Within a year Massine had created his first ballet *Soleil de Nuit* which was a series of Russian dances to the music of Rimsky-Korsakov. In 1917 in Rome came *Le Femmes de Bonne Humeur (The Good-Humoured Ladies)*. This was a complicated story of disguises and mistaken identities, danced to the music of Scarlatti, with décor by Bakst.

Massine was developing fast both as a dancer and a choreographer. His would never be a great classical dancer for his legs were too short, but he had a tremendous stage presence and was very skilled at dramatic character parts.

As a choreographer he was an expressionist and very much a man of his time. Where Nijinsky's approach had been slow, intense and emotional,

Massine's was fast and fun. Often grotesque and satiric, it matched the mood of the day. Within a short time he reached the peak of his early development with two of his finest ballets *La Boutique Fantasque* and *Le Tricorne (The Three-cornered Hat)*, both presented in London in 1919.

The war was over, theatre lights were coming up again and early in the year Diaghilev brought his Ballets Russes to England. Though most of the company were new there were some familiar faces from the old days. The faithful stage manager Grigoriev was there with his wife Tchernicheva, a dancer from the Maryinksy. Karsavina returned and so did the mercurial Lydia Lopokova, who had flitted in and out of Diaghilev's life like a butterfly. His other Lydia, the faithful Sokolova alias Hilda Munnings, was also with him again and he had found two splendid male dancers from the school in Warsaw: Stanislas Idzikowsky and Leon Woizikovsky who was a tower of strength for the type of role previously danced by Adolph Bolm.

La Boutique Fantasque had its premiere at the Alhambra Theatre in June with the enchanting Lopokova in the leading role, partnered by Massine. It was a truly international offering with Russian dancers on an English stage in a ballet based on an old German story, danced to the music of an Italian composer Rossini, in a décor by a French artist Derain! This was the beginning of a

OVERLEAF
LEFT *La Boutique Fantasque (The Fantastic Toyshop)* was Massine's up-dated version of the German classic *The Fairy Doll*. He danced the leading role partnering Lopokova at the ballet's première in London in 1919. This production is by the Royal Ballet. (*Mike Davis Studios, Jesse Davis*)

RIGHT *The Three-Cornered Hat (Le Tricorne)* was one of Massine's earliest and most successful creations as choreographer and leading dancer. The ballet has passed into the repertoire of many companies today; this shows a Festival Ballet production. (*Mike Davis Studios, Jesse Davis*)

new trend. Diaghilev was to surround himself more and more with the international avant-garde set, and Derain was the first of the French easel artists to work for him.

For *Le Tricorne* Diaghilev commissioned the Spanish painter Pablo Picasso, who created a set that brilliantly captured the arid sunbaked atmosphere of a Spanish village, matching the mood of de Falla's fiery music. The story is a simple one. A jealous miller has a beautiful wife who is pursued by an elderly *corregidor* who plans to seduce her, but he is successfully outwitted.

Karsavina created the role of the miller's lovely wife, but the high spot was Massine dancing his famous *Flamenco Farruca* – a traditional gipsy dance that he had brilliantly recreated in ballet terms, and which exactly suited his temperament.

Massine was now 23 years old. In four years he had produced seven full-length ballets, working at speed under great tension. The first flush of creative genius was over. He needed time to rest and re-charge his batteries, but the demands of the Ballets Russes were still pressing. He was their only choreographer and Diaghilev had just set him a

The set for the original production of *The Three-Cornered Hat* in 1919 was by Picasso. Massine is seen here on stage, dancing the part of the Miller. (*Mander & Mitchenson Theatre Collection*)

task that showed a curious lapse of judgement. He asked Massine to revive *Le Sacre du Printemps*.

Massine was quite unfitted by temperament and inclination to deal with this folklore theme of mystery, fear and tragedy. He found it a great strain and his version that went into the 1920 repertoire did nothing for the ballet or Stravinsky's music, though it probably produced some better moments of theatre.

Diaghilev followed this error of judgement with another far more cataclysmic one. In 1921 he decided to launch in London a full-scale revival of *The Sleeping Beauty* which he called *The Sleeping Princess*. He was setting out to recreate the great days of classical ballet and perhaps, as some have suggested, recapture his own lost youth and memories of his beloved Russia.

There was also another, more urgent reason. He had no choreographer. After *Le Sacre* Massine had left him. He wanted to get married and he did not intend to follow Nijinsky's example and wait around to be dismissed. Like Nijinsky he married a dancer from the company, and they went off to South America.

Diaghilev, lonely and deeply depressed, plunged into his new venture. As usual with him it had to be done on the grand scale. He signed a contract for a long season at the Alhambra Theatre with Sir Oswald Stoll, who advanced a large sum of money

This picture from the 1921 production of *The Sleeping Princess* shows the wicked fairy Carabosse danced by 54-year-old Carlotta Brianza. As ballerina of the Maryinsky she had created the role of Princess Aurora at the ballet's premiere thirty-one years earlier. (*London, Victoria and Albert Museum*)

to cover expenses. The debts piled up as Diaghilev assembled a huge company and set his old friend Léon Bakst to work to redesign the elaborate sets and hundreds of costumes.

Diaghilev himself travelled all over Europe to track down the dancers he wanted. He assembled an astonishing array of talent, including three great ballerinas from the old Maryinsky to share the role of Aurora: Vera Trefilova, now 46 years old and teaching in her own school in Paris; Lubov Egorova, now 41 years old, and Olga Spessivtseva, 26 years old and still at the Maryinsky, who obtained permission to come as guest artist. He even tracked down the original Aurora, Carlotta Brianza, now 54 years old and teaching in Paris. She came to take the part of the Fairy Carabosse –

a role taken over for one night by 71-year-old Cecchetti to celebrate his golden jubilee as a dancer. To augment the *corps de ballet* Diaghilev engaged English dancers including an athletic, talented young man of seventeen, who was being trained in the Maryinsky tradition by Astafieva in her London school. His name was Patrick Kay, later he was to be known to the world as Anton Dolin.

Diaghilev geared himself for a first night triumph. He even invited over to England the leading French critics to witness his success. Alas for him, the first night was a near disaster. The stage machinery failed to work properly, and there were long delays while stage hands struggled with the cumbersome sets. The atmosphere of the ballet was wrecked and the audience became rude and restive. Diaghilev was reduced to tears.

'Business will pick up,' his friends consoled him. But it did not. The music of Tchaikovsky had lost its appeal for ears now tuned to the strident discords of modern composers, while an ancient fairy tale meant nothing to the sophisticated theatre-goers of the '20s. They were running at a loss. Debts were piling up and finally they were forced to close long before the end of the season. Sets and costumes were impounded, and Diaghilev was left bankrupt.

A sketch for the original production of *Les Noces* by Russian artist Natalia Goncharova, who designed the costumes and sets which captured the authentic spirit of this Russian peasant wedding evoked by Stravinsky's music and Nijinska's choreography. It is interesting to note how closely the Royal Ballet production follows the original. (*London, Victoria and Albert Museum*)

RIGHT Nijinsky's sister Nijinska created *Les Noces* for Diaghilev in 1923. It has been rated as one of her most important works, and is still performed by many companies. This photograph shows a scene from the recent Royal Ballet production. (*Mike Davis Studios, Jesse Davis*)

Exhausted and shocked, he came near to total defeat. To him it seemed the world had rejected his supreme offering of Russian beauty, art and music. By now Diaghilev was nearly 50 and his health was already being undermined by the diabetes that was to kill him. He had only another eight years to live but in that short time this astonishing man was to achieve a new wave of success with a series of experimental modern ballets. These are usually labelled 'Diaghilev's cocktail period', and experts have written them off as trivial, theatre-filling novelties designed to catch a passing fashion. Though many of them deserved

The birth of a great partnership: Anton Dolin and Alicia Markova joined Diaghilev's Ballets Russes in 1923 and 1925 when he was 19 and she was 15. They are seen here together in *Les Biches*. (*John Topham Picture Library*)

TOP *Les Biches*, meaning in effect 'The Bright Young Things' of the '20s, was produced by Nijinska in January 1924. The theme is a house party for the smart set in the South of France. This picture shows a scene from the original production. (*Mander & Mitchenson Theatre Collection*)

LEFT Nijinska's choreography for *The Blue Train*, based on beach games and sports like swimming and tennis, reflects the light hearted activities of chic society on a Mediterranean beach. The dancers are Sokolova, Dolin, Nijinska and Woizikovsky. (*BBC Hulton Picture Library*)

this judgement and have sunk without a trace, some have survived and have come to be seen in perspective as valuable early works by developing choreographers.

The most important thing about Diaghilev in the '20s was that he provided a launching pad for a whole new generation of dancers and choreographers who have been, and still are, shaping the ballet of today.

His headquarters in Monte Carlo became once more a power house of new ideas as Diaghilev surrounded himself with another avant-garde group, only this time they were mainly French. His old friend Jean Cocteau, the writer and designer, was now a constant companion, as were the composers François Poulenc and Georges Auric, whose ideas had been shaped by Eric Satie, one of the seminal influences of twentieth-century music. His scores are still heard today in many contemporary ballets, including those of Merce Cunningham. With the expressionist painters Georges Braque and Marie Laurencin, and Nijinsky's sister Bronislava, they formed the inner cabinet known as 'The Six'. Nijinska was the only Russian. She had rejoined Diaghilev for *The Sleeping Princess*, replacing Cecchetti as ballet master, and she remained to become his only woman choreographer.

One of the first ballets she did for him was Diaghilev's last nostalgic look at the Russia of his youth. *Les Noces* is a celebration of a traditional peasant wedding. With Stravinsky's music and Goncharova's scenery and costumes, Nijinska created a work of deep religious feeling and with an intensely Russian atmosphere. This was an expressionist ballet stemming directly from her brother's *Sacre*, and showing also the strong influence of the Dalcroze rhythmic theories. *Les Noces* had its premiere in Paris in 1923, and has lived on. It is regarded as one of Nijinska's masterpieces.

She followed this by a ballet in complete contrast, firmly set in the France of the 1920s, *Les Biches* (which means 'the young hinds' or, colloquially, 'the little darlings'). These are a set of bright young things at a smart house party in the South of France. The music of Poulenc created the jazz flavour of the time, matched by Laurencin's sets. For Nijinska this was a transitional ballet in which she was moving from the now out-dated expressionist ballet to a pseudo-classical style in which traditional dancing is brought into line with modern music and décor by the use of sophisticated, distorted movements. *Les Biches* was fun, satirical and modern, and Paris loved it.

Diaghilev was now collecting the new talent he needed for these new-style ballets. Among the first to join the company in 1923 was Astafieva's pupil Pat Kay, now Anton Dolin, in whom Diaghilev saw a leading male dancer of the future. Dolin combined athletic strength with classical grace and the lively temperament of his Irish ancestry. In fact it was his interest in acrobatics that led to the creation of the ballet that was to rocket him to fame. Jean Cocteau came across him one day in the studio in Monte Carlo, fooling about doing handstands and backflips. It gave him the idea for a new ballet: the result was *The Blue Train*. The ballet has no plot, it simply shows the smart set having fun and games on a Riviera beach led by 'Le Beau Gosse'.

Nijinska's clever choreography gave Anton Dolin the opportunity for some spectacular acrobatics carried out with the grace and elegance of a classical dancer. Diaghilev launched him in Paris in great style with music by Milhaud, a curtain by Picasso and costumes by leading fashion designer Coco Chanel. *The Blue Train* had its premiere at Le Théâtre de Champs-Elysées on 20 June 1924. It was a triumph and 19-year-old Anton Dolin was on his way, though the ballet itself has completely dropped out of sight.

Another dancer from England had arrived about the same time as Dolin. Irish-born Ninette de Valois joined the company as a soloist in 1923 when she was 25 years old. She had been a pupil of Espinosa, Legat and Cecchetti and now she was adding Nijinska's teaching to her assorted training. This wide-ranging experience of different classical styles was to stand her in good stead for here was not a ballerina of the future but the founder of the English school of ballet on the threshold of her great career.

The other new arrival of 1923 was an unknown young Russian who arrived unannounced with a group of four dancers whom Diaghilev had 'ordered' from Nijinska's school in Kiev. Serge Lifar had taken the place of a dancer who had dropped out. Virtually untrained, he had no business to be there, but Diaghilev saw in this incredibly handsome young man another Massine or Nijinsky. Instead of sending him back, he sent him on to Cecchetti in Milan. The great maestro's

Once cast aside as a dated, trivial piece from Diaghilev's 'cocktail' period, *Les Biches* has been rediscovered and revalued in recent years and is shown here performed by the Royal Ballet. (*Mike Davis Studios, Jesse Davis*)

Monte Carlo, 1925. Left to right: 1, Madame Cecchetti; 2 Doubrovska; 3, Markova; 4-7, unknown; 8, de Valois; 9, Sokolova; 10, unknown; 11, Soumarokova; 12, Chamie; 13, Woizikowsky; 14, Lifar; 15, Tcherkas; 16, Nikitina; 17, Dolin, 18 Danilova; 19, unknown; 20, Savina; 21 Cecchetti.

A unique assembly of talent in 1925 in the rehearsal room of the theatre at Monte Carlo, where the Ballets Russes spent their winters rehearsing and training under their great ballet master Enrico Cecchetti, now 75 years old. He dedicated this picture to his pupil, 15-year-old Alice Marks (Alicia Markova). (*London, Victoria and Albert Museum*)

teaching could not make up for the lack of training in the formative years, but Lifar worked incredibly hard and made astonishing progress. He also developed a tremendous stage personality.

1925 found Diaghilev in Paris again, auditioning some Soviet dancers who had been touring Germany. Their leader was a young man called George Balanchivadze, better known today as Balanchine. Born in St. Petersburg in 1904, he had entered the Imperial school at 10 years old and

received the full classical training, graduating with honours in 1921. Young, talented and eager to experiment with the expressionist trends of the day, he found the way in Russia blocked by the establishment and this tour of Germany was his bid for freedom. Diaghilev engaged him together with two of his fellow graduates Alexandra Danilova and Tamara Geva, whom Balanchine had married.

Though Diaghilev was aware that in Balanchine he had acquired a choreographer of the future, there was still the present to contend with. Nijinska had left him after some differences of opinion, but fortunately Massine was within reach for he had returned to Paris. His wife had already returned to the company after a divorce. Massine, having established his independence, was willing to come under contract as Diaghilev's choreographer. The result was *Les Matelots*, a light-hearted nautical romp which had its premiere at the London Coliseum in June 1925 and launched Lifar into stardom.

The following season the Balanchine ballets began to flow: *Jack in the Box*, a short *divertissement* with music by Satie, and a full-length ballet *The Triumph of Neptune* in pseudo-classical style, based somewhat inaccurately on the English Christmas pantomime tradition. In 1926 Balanchine also re-created a charming short ballet *Le Rossignol (The Nightingale)* to launch a very young dancer who had just joined the company, 15-year-old Alice Marks, who had been Anton Dolin's fellow pupil under Astafieva, and whom Diaghilev presented to the world as Alicia Markova.

From then on Balanchine dominated the scene. Nijinska returned briefly in 1926 to give *Romeo and Juliet* the cocktail ballet treatment, with Karsavina

and Dolin in the leading roles, but this was her last work for Diaghilev. She went on to join Ida Rubinstein who had started up her own company in Paris.

Massine produced *Le Pas d'Acier*, a ballet depicting life in a soviet factory to music by Prokofiev, followed by *Ode*. In complete contrast, this was a meditation on the wonders of nature based on a text by an eighteenth century Russian poet. It was an abstract ballet, and its main interest lay in the use made of special lighting and film projection techniques that were still in the experimental stage.

Balanchine's new ballet that season *La Chatte* also explored new stage effects by using a constructivist décor. This one, made entirely of transparent materials, produced some remarkable lighting effects. The story of *La Chatte*, based on Aesop's fable, provided a brilliant role for Lifar. Balanchine was now getting into his stride, and the flow of his great ballets began.

In 1928 *Apollon Musagète (Apollo)* with a score by Stravinsky appeared, and *Les Dieux Mendiants (The Gods go a-Begging)* to Handel's music, arranged by Sir Thomas Beecham, had its premiere in London. In 1929 came *The Prodigal Son* to Prokofiev's score with a décor by the French artist Rouault. This ballet, based on the Bible story, brought together a

In 1927 Massine created *La Chatte*, a ballet based on Aesop's fable in which a cat, beloved by a young man, is turned into a girl. But she soon becomes more interested in a mouse and returns to her old cat-self again. With a set made of new transparent, light-reflecting materials and ultra modern choreography, the ballet displayed Serge Lifar's talents admirably. (*Mander & Mitchenson Theatre Collection*)

The Prodigal Son was one of Diaghilev's last ballets, appearing in May 1929, only three months before he died. It introduced a new and brilliant young choreographer to the world, George Balanchine. The dancers here are from the Royal Ballet. (*Mike Davis Studios, Jesse Davis*)

splendid quartet of male talent with Balanchine, Lifar, Dolin and Woizikovsky. Finally there was *Le Bal*, with Anton Dolin partnering Sokolova.

The company were at Covent Garden and the whole of the 1929 season had been a triumph, with packed houses and ringing applause. But Diaghilev was hearing it for the last time. By now he was a very sick man, and when the season ended and the company scattered on holiday, he returned to his beloved Venice, accompanied by his faithful secretary Boris Kochno and the devoted Lifar. In his hotel bedroom he lay in a high fever until a diabetic coma brought unconsciousness and death. As though nature herself was aware of the final curtain of this great man of the theatre, a dramatic storm broke out over the lagoon as he died. He lies buried on the Island of San Michele.

Diaghilev had gone but his legacy to ballet was to continue in the lives of Massine, de Valois, Dolin, Markova, Lifar and Balanchine, who were to carry their great heritage into France, England and America, and from there into the far corners of the world. From this time onward each country was to develop its own story of the ballet.

6
Britain

The Russian seeds sown in English soil since the beginning of the century were growing vigorously by the 1920s as dancers and teachers set up their schools.

In London in 1918 Cecchetti and his wife opened their ballet school, which was to lead to the foundation of the Cecchetti Society, whose aim was to perpetuate his methods. That same year, the legendary Karsavina, now married to an English diplomat Henry Bruce, made London her home and passed on to privileged pupils her treasure store of knowledge.

In 1920 Serafina Astafieva opened her school in Nottinghill Gate and six years later one of the great St. Petersburg teachers Nicolas Legat, who had succeeded Johansson as Director of the Imperial Academy, made London his home and opened a school in Hammersmith.

One other name also prominent on the teaching scene in those days was that of Edouard Espinosa, the son of Spanish-born Léon Espinosa who had trained in the Paris Opéra and gone on to become leading dancer in the Bolshoi Theatre, Moscow before settling in London in 1872, and founding a school. Edouard, a fine professional dancer himself, had carried on his father's work and become a much-sought-after teacher.

It was Espinosa's concern for the ballet that led to the creation, in December 1920, of the Association of Operatic Dancing, which later became the Royal Academy of Dancing (RAD). Its purpose was, and still is, to watch over the standards of teaching, and today its examinations are recognized throughout the world. To help launch his new scheme, Espinosa enlisted the help of fellow dancers Karsavina and Adeline Genée. This vivacious and charming Danish dancer had been a regular visitor to London ever since she first appeared as a 19-year-old at Queen Victoria's Diamond Jubilee in 1897. Genée had become London's favourite ballerina at the Empire Theatre

This picture, taken in 1908 when she was at the height of her popularity with London audiences, shows Adeline Genée as Swanilda in *Coppélia*. Later she helped to establish British ballet, was honoured and made a Dame, and presided over the Royal Academy for thirty years. (*London, Victoria and Albert Museum*)

all through the Edwardian years and by this time England was her home and she had become a leading personality in the ballet scene. She gave her unfailing support to struggling British ballet and for thirty years she was president of RAD. Today, the Genée Theatre in Sussex is a tribute to her memory.

Though the names of the great ballerinas added lustre to the project, it was someone from the other side of the footlights who was really the driving force in establishing the academy. Philip Richardson, writer and tireless propagandist for the dance, was editor of *The Dancing Times*, and through the pages of his magazine he began campaigning for the establishment of a British national ballet. The future of this idea lay in the hands of two formidable women, now known as Dame Marie Rambert, and Dame Ninette de Valois.

Marie Rambert was the first to go into action. England had become her home since her marriage to the writer Ashley Dukes in 1918, but domesticity and the care of two baby daughters did not satisfy her. Hers was a restless, active, pioneering spirit and so, helped and encouraged by her husband, she opened a school of dancing and collected her first group of pupils. In 1927 she and her husband managed to buy an old church hall in Nottinghill Gate and turned it into a studio and stage for 'Marie Rambert Dancers', amongst whom was a solitary man, the 19-year-old Frederick Ashton. His desire to dance had been kindled years before when, as a boy in South America, he had seen Pavlova dance in Lima. The impression she made on him was to shape his life. However, it was a secret that he had to keep from his conventional parents. His father, a business man, had strict ideas about a boy's upbringing, and young Frederick had to endure English boarding school followed by captivity in a London office. He did, however, manage to start weekly dancing lessons with Massine. Freedom came at last when his father died, and Massine introduced him to Marie Rambert. Now, in her skilled hands his true life's work could begin.

Although his lack of early training barred the way to great achievement as a classical dancer, he had a true gift for mime and she was quick to dis-

Lady into Fox was created in 1939 by Andrée Howard, one of Rambert's most promising dancers and choreographers, who left the company to go to America with Anthony Tudor. The leading role of Silvia was created by Sally Gilmour, seen here partnered by Charles Boyd. (*London, Victoria and Albert Museum*)

Two more pioneers of British ballet in 1926: Anton Dolin, who was to form the Festival Ballet, and Ninette de Valois, founder of the Vic-Wells, now the Royal Ballet. They are seen here in Dolin's ballet *Little Boy Blue*. (*Mander & Mitchenson Theatre Collection*)

cover his even greater gift for choreography and to encourage it. The first Ashton ballet *A Tragedy of Fashion* went into a review at the Lyric Theatre, Hammersmith, and ran for several months. Later, the opportunity came for Ashton to join the company newly formed by Ida Rubinstein in Paris, and Marie Rambert urged him to go. For two years he had the experience of dancing and working under Massine and Nijinska.

By the time he returned to the studio in Nottinghill, the Marie Rambert Dancers were poised for a new entrance as 'The Ballet Club'. Marie's years of dedicated teaching were bringing their reward; her pupils were turning into professional performers, and they now included other male dancers destined to make their mark: Harold Turner, from Manchester; Walter Gore from Scotland and a remarkable young man, William Cook, who had been coming to train in the Rambert studio at the end of a 10-hour working day in an accountant's office in the Smithfield meat market. The world was to know him as Antony Tudor. Another young choreographer in the making was Andrée Howard, who had come from the great Maryinsky teachers in Paris, Egorova and Preobrajenska.

These were exhilarating days for the young dancers and their dynamic teacher. Though Marie was a severe disciplinarian in the classroom, she never failed to encourage her pupils. The Ballet Club flourished and, before long, the church hall evolved into a small theatre complex when Marie and her husband acquired two adjoining houses and converted them into rehearsal rooms and dressing rooms. In 1933 they proudly launched The Mercury Theatre, and here, on its tiny stage that measured only 5.5 metres (18ft) across, many British choreographers of the future and potential leading dancers made their débuts.

In the meantime Ninette de Valois had also been busy. After leaving Diaghilev in 1926 she opened her school in South Kensington, London under the grand name of the 'Academy of Choreographic Art'. That same year she had the good fortune to meet Lilian Baylis, pioneer of British drama and opera, who was running the Old Vic Theatre near Waterloo station. She happened to be looking for someone to teach her actors to move and to arrange dances, so a great partnership got under way. Their common aim was to establish British national ballet, and together they faced the uphill struggle to achieve it.

The arrival of the dancers gave Lilian Baylis fresh incentive to follow through her plan to have a

In 1937 Ninette de Valois produced *Checkmate* for the Vic-Wells Ballet. It has had frequent revivals; this picture shows Monica Mason as the Black Queen and Nureyev as the Red Knight in a recent production of this dramatic ballet, which is danced on the black and white squares of a giant chessboard. (*Mike Davis Studios, Jesse Davis*)

second theatre in north London. Islington had long been a playground for Londoners and one of the oldest Victorian music halls was still there on the site of an old mineral spring that a man called Sadler had developed in the seventeenth century as a watering place and pleasure garden. Here, Lilian Baylis built the Sadler's Wells Theatre. It opened in 1931 and Ninette de Valois and her

dancers moved in: the Vic-Wells company had been born. British ballet was gathering momentum, and more help was coming from another source.

The Camargo Society, started in 1930, had come into existence to try and fill the gap left in ballet-goers lives by the death of Diaghilev. Once again, that champion of the ballet, Philip Richardson, was the driving force behind it with fellow-writer and critic Arnold Haskell, who was a dedicated balletomane. Their immediate purpose was to finance productions on Diaghilev lines using home-trained talent.

Old friends rallied round: Genée, Karsavina, Lopokova (now married to the economist Lord Keynes), Nicolas Legat, Anton Dolin and Alicia Markova. Enthusiasts from the wealthier strata of society gave generous support and the Camargo Society got under way with Sunday evening performances in any theatre they could hire. This is how one of Ashton's most popular ballets came to see the light of day, for *Façade* had its premiere at the Cambridge Theatre in 1931. It was an immediate success, and has passed into the permanent repertoire of the Royal Ballet where it remains a favourite with the public.

The de Valois ballet, *Job*, also had its premiere that same year. Based on the William Blake illustrations from the Old Testament book, it depicts Job's unshakeable belief in God, against which even Satan cannot prevail. This was an important work because

Façade, one of Frederick Ashton's first ballets, consists of a series of satirical sketches to music by William Walton. It was put on by the Camargo Society in 1931. Immediately successful, it has remained one of his most popular works. This picture of the Ballet Rambert production shows Margot Fonteyn with Robert Helpmann kneeling on the left, and Ashton lying down in the centre. (*London, Royal Opera House Archives*)

it developed a new trend. Ninette de Valois had been forced to create dances in free-style movement because the composer Vaughan Williams had made it a condition for his music that it should not be called a ballet, and that there should be no point work – a technique he detested. As a result, de Valois created a powerful evocation of Blake's pictures in movement and grouping, and the stage was dominated by Satan, magnificently danced by Anton Dolin.

It was out of these Camargo days that the great Markova-Dolin partnership was born. They became the leading dancers at the Vic-Wells in its early years, and it was because of their already wide experience that de Valois was able to build up

The Rake's Progress, rated as one of Ninette de Valois's best works, had its premiere in 1935. Her new Vic-Wells company had just captured two of Rambert's best dancers, Walter Gore, seen here as the Rake and Harold Turner, seen as the Dancing Master. (*London, Royal Opera House Archives*)

Lithuanian-born Alexis Rassine joined the Vic-Wells company in the war years and became their leading dancer. He is seen here in *Giselle*, partnering Moira Shearer, who had emerged from the Sadler's Wells school to be appointed ballerina in 1944. (*London, Royal Opera House Archives*)

an impressive classical repertoire. The choreography for this came directly from the Maryinsky Theatre. De Valois was lucky enough to enlist the help of a key man Nicholas Sergeyev, who had been stage manager there in pre-war days. When he left Russia in 1918 he had taken with him the precious notebooks in which he had recorded most of the great ballets in the repertoire. Now, through him, the young Vic-Wells company were able to recreate them one by one.

The de Valois policy, however, had always been to create new British ballets alongside the classics. Having, as yet, no choreographer she set to work to do it herself. The results were such ballets as *The*

Rudolf Nureyev produced a new version of the *Nutcracker* for the Royal Ballet in 1968. He is seen here in the part of Drosselmayer. (*Mike Davis Studios, Jesse Davis*)

LEFT Two Canadian-born stars of the Royal Ballet, Lynn Seymour and Wayne Eagling dancing in MacMillan's ballet *The Invitation*, first produced in 1960. (*Mike Davis Studios, Jesse Davis*)

Haunted Ballroom with music by Geoffrey Toye, which gave the world its first glimpse of a 15-year-old dancer who was to become the company's greatest star – Margot Fonteyn. There was also *The Rake's Progress*, one of de Valois's finest works, in which she recreated the bawdy eighteenth-century London life shown in Hogarth's series of paintings. The leading role was created by Walter Gore who had just joined the company.

This was the beginning of a steady stream of talent moving from Rambert to de Valois, for the Mercury Theatre was too small and too financially precarious to be able to hold its developing talent. Walter Gore was followed by Harold Turner in 1935, and that same year, the biggest prize of all Frederick Ashton, joined the company. The great days were beginning as the stream of Ashton choreographic invention began to flow.

New pupils also were emerging from the school, and when Markova and Dolin left in 1935 to start

Helpmann's talent as a choreographer developed during the years of World War II. One of his best-known ballets is *Hamlet*, dating from 1942, with Helpmann himself seen here in the leading role. (*London, Royal Opera House Archives*)

RIGHT Two promising pupils emerged from the Vic-Wells school in the 1930s, to take the leading roles in the classical ballets: Margot Fonteyn, and Robert Helpmann. They are seen here in *The Sleeping Princess*, a triumphant production to celebrate the company's move to the Royal Opera House in 1946. (*London, Victoria and Albert Museum*)

their own company, their places were taken by young Fonteyn and a new arrival from Australia Robert Helpmann. He had only been with the company a year and had very little training, but he rapidly developed into a dancer of extraordinary versatility, combining classical roles with a remarkable talent for mime and comedy.

Fonteyn was to become Ashton's great inspiration. He found in her the perfect interpreter of his work, and together they headed the team that was building up the company's reputation with ballets that were to become box office favourites: *Apparitions* (1936), *Les Patineurs* (1937) and *Horoscope* (1938).

The Camargo Society, having seen its purpose fulfilled, quietly folded up and withdrew. Lilian Baylis also had the satisfaction of seeing the young company on its way before she died in 1937.

This was the year that the Vic-Wells achieved another milestone. They gave their first season in Paris. At the Théâtre de Champs-Elysées, scene of so many Diaghilev trimphs, Ninette de Valois saw her own British company win over Paris audiences, who were delighted with the newcomers. She also launched her own ballet *Checkmate*, danced on a gigantic chess board. Robert Helpmann as the Red King gave a dance-mime performance that has never been surpassed.

World War II brought tough times and a battering as the Sadler's Wells Theatre was damaged by bombs. The company not only managed to keep going, however, but became an important part of the country's cultural life through these years of survival. It also changed its name from the Vic-Wells to the Sadler's Wells Ballet.

Many male dancers left for war service, but the company was helped out by Lithuanian-born Alexis Rassine, who came to them via South Africa and Paris, where he had studied with Preobrajenska. He took over many of the classical roles and also created roles in new ballets by Robert Helpmann who was beginning to emerge as a choreographer. His first ballet *Comus* had its premiere in 1942, followed by *Hamlet* and *Miracle in the Gorbals*, which was a morality play set in the slums of Glasgow.

By the time the war ended the idea had taken root that the state should help support the arts. When Covent Garden Opera House was reopened as a theatre in 1946, with the help of what is now the Arts Council, the Sadler's Wells Ballet was invited to become its first resident company. They celebrated the move into their new home with a magnificent full-length revival of *The Sleeping Beauty*. This time Diaghilev's 1921 disaster turned into a triumph and set the seal of success on the company's new status. Ninette de Valois had achieved her ambition and established the first British national ballet, though ten years were to pass before the final accolade in 1956, when the royal charter was granted and it became the Royal Ballet.

Throughout all this time Margot Fonteyn continued unrivalled as the top ballerina. She had by

Antoinette Sibley and Anthony Dowell formed one of the great partnerships of the Royal Ballet. Here they are seen as Titania and Oberon in *The Dream*, Frederick Ashton's ballet based on *A Midsummer Night's Dream*. (*John Topham Picture Library*)

then been dancing leading roles for nearly twenty years, and the shadow of retirement was beginning to fall across her path when, suddenly, there came into her life a young dancer who was to launch her on a second career. Rudolf Nureyev, trained in the Leningrad school, had left the Kirov ballet during a Paris season in 1961 and requested political asylum in France. He found a niche in the Grand Ballet du Marquis de Cuevas where Rambert's Peggy van Praagh became his first western-style teacher. Fonteyn invited him to London for a gala performance and from this stemmed an astonishing partnership between the 42-year-old ballerina and the 23-year-old Russian dancer, whose dazzling virtuosity and tremendous stage presence captured everyone's imagination and gave the world a new image of the male dancer.

Sally Owen and Gianfranco Paoluzzi of the Ballet Rambert dancing in Christopher Bruce's *Night with Waning Moon*. (*Mike Davis Studios, Jesse Davis*)

LEFT The new Ballet Rambert presented Glen Tetley's spectacular production of *The Tempest* in 1979, with Gianfranco Paoluzzi as Ariel. (*Mike Davis Studios, Jesse Davis*)

For the next ten years Fonteyn and Nureyev danced as guest stars with companies all over the world. Through television they brought their art into the homes of millions and one of their most popular mass-media works was the film of *Le Corsaire* in 1964.

By this time other new dancers were reaching the top in the Royal Ballet: Merle Parke, Canadian-born Lynn Seymour, and Anthony Dowell, whose partnership with Antoinette Sibley produced some

moments of brilliant artistry.

Dame Ninette de Valois retired as director in 1963, handing over to Sir Frederick Ashton who carried on her work, and whose special achievement was to make the *corps de ballet* one of the finest in the world.

Since 1970 Kenneth MacMillan has directed the company and has added to the repertoire many fine works of his own, such as *Anastasia* in 1971 and *Manon* and *Elite Syncopations* in 1974. He has consistently extended the company's powers, and their repertoire today has an astonishing range.

By contrast, Marie Rambert and her company had a more difficult time. Being a pioneer rather than the founder of an establishment, it was inevitable that others would reap the rewards of her work. Losing Ashton, Turner and Gore was bad enough, though Gore did return later and remained with the company for many years, but then in 1938 she lost Antony Tudor, who left to form his own London Ballet company, taking with him Andrée Howard and most of the best dancers.

This was a blow from which the company never really recovered. When the war started Tudor and Howard went to America and a merger produced the London-Rambert company directed by Peggy van Praagh. This was disbanded in 1941 and it was not until 1943 that Marie was able to start again with her own Ballet Rambert. This time she had financial help from the state godparent the Arts Council, and her company spent the rest of the war touring garrisons and factories. They were among

John Gilpin became the Festival Ballet's leading dancer and directed the company from 1962–1965. He is seen here in *Vision of Marguerite*, a revised version of Ashton's *Mephisto Valse*. (*John Topham Picture Library*)

OPPOSITE The great Markova-Dolin partnership launched the new Festival Ballet company at the Stoll Theatre London in 1950. They are seen here in *Swan Lake*. (*London Festival Ballet*)

the first to tour in Germany in 1946 and the following year saw them in Australia and New Zealand. In 1957 they went to China, and in 1959 they were in the United States where Marie saw Martha Graham dance for the first time and was completely captivated. The idea of contemporary dance took root in the company, and it is this which has developed and transformed it.

New choreographic talent began to emerge with Norman Morrice who joined the company in 1951 and scored a success in America in 1958 with his first ballet *The Two Brothers*. This tells of the rivalry between two brothers for a girl, and ends with a murder. Seen as a contemporary social situation, it was the first British ballet seriously to present this type of theme. Christopher Bruce and John Chesworth were also developing choreographically in a modern direction, and all three were moving away from classical ballets such as *Giselle* and *Swan Lake*.

The moment of change came in 1966 when the company finally shed its connection with classical ballet and re-formed itself as a small, forward-looking experimental group, with Marie Rambert and Norman Morrice becoming co-directors in 1970. The adrenalin began to flow once more and new ballets literally poured out – fifty of them in the first ten years. The company received a further powerful impetus with the arrival of American Glen Tetley, who created some of his most important works for them.

Glen Tetley had his first break-through as a choreographer in New York with *Pierrot Lunaire* in 1962 and had since worked as a freelance in Europe. His dancing background had ranged from contemporary with Martha Graham and Jerome Robbins, to classical with the American Theater Ballet. He had also spent two years as director of the Stuttgart Ballet, succeeding John Cranko. During this time his choreography, that had started out uncompromisingly modern, began to show classical influences, and this has given rise to the unique Tetley blend of styles that, in turn, has given the Ballet Rambert its own distinctive identity.

In 1979 Tetley produced his first full-length ballet for them: *The Tempest*. Treating Shakespeare's theme as mainly symbolic, he created a powerful evocation of Prospero's island, where his bare-foot dancers dramatically combined beautiful classical elevation, precision and speed with contemporary 'fall and recovery', matched by Arne Nordheim's music that moved from the melodic lines of Ariel's song to theatre-shaking percussion discords. This fusion of dance and music was in a setting by Nadine

LEFT The Festival Ballet's production of *Romeo and Juliet*, with Nureyev and Patricia Ruanne. The sets, on a grand scale, are by Ezio Frigerio. (*London Festival Ballet, Anthony Crickmay*)

Baylis – a regular interpreter of Tetley's ideas – that added the final dimension to a production that achieved moments of great theatre.

By this time, Marie Rambert, now in her nineties, could perhaps feel reassured that, in the safe hands of its director Christopher Bruce and his assistant John Chesworth, her company would go on.

The classics remained with the only other large touring company, the London Festival Ballet. This had grown out of the original Markova-Dolin partnership and was launched in October 1950 at the Stoll Theatre with a glittering array of stars that included Massine and Riabouchinska of the Ballets Russes days, and a very promising young dancer John Gilpin, who took over Dolin's roles when he retired. He also became artistic director of the company for a short time before Beryl Grey took over in 1968.

As the company had to pay its own way, it had to

In 1979 the Danish dancer Peter Schaufuss recreated *La Sylphide* for the Festival Ballet, using the original Bournonville choreography. He is seen here dancing with guest artist Eva Evdokimova, the Danish ballerina. (*London Festival Ballet, Anthony Crickmay*)

LEFT Nureyev also produced a magnificent *Sleeping Beauty* for the Festival Ballet in 1975. (*Mike Davis Studios, Jesse Davis*)

The Scottish Ballet's production of the Bournonville classic *Napoli*, Act III. (*Scottish National Ballet, William Cooper*)

rely on the popular appeal of well-established ballets, and guest stars with box office drawing power. Nureyev produced a magnificent *Sleeping Beauty* for them in 1975 and, more recently in 1979, a young Danish dancer Peter Schaufuss from Copenhagen, produced *La Sylphide* in the true Bournonville tradition. He scored a double triumph with his choreography and his own superb dancing in the leading role.

Regular London seasons, usually at the Royal Festival Hall, were followed by long tours in England and overseas and in this way the company built up a solid following. Beryl Grey resigned in 1979 and was succeeded by her former partner of Sadler's Wells days John Field. A fine classical dancer and a man of wide experience, he had already built up the Royal Ballet's young touring company at Sadler's Wells and was a director of

RAD. His appointment was a popular one with the company.

Outside London there has also been a growth of regional dance companies, including the Northern Ballet Theatre and the Scottish Ballet. This started life in Bristol as the Western Ballet, founded by Elizabeth West, an Espinosa pupil, and Peter Darrell who was trained at Sadler's Wells. When Elizabeth died in a climbing accident in 1962, he found himself in sole charge and continued as director, fighting a tough struggle for survival.

He too was a choreographer in the contemporary manner. The themes of many of his ballets, such as *The Prisoners* (1957) and *Mods and Rockers* (1963) to the music of the Beatles, reflect his concern with current social conditions. When the company moved to Glasgow in 1969 they renamed themselves the Scottish Ballet, and Peter Darrell has continued with them, building up an impressive repertoire of modern experimental works to encourage new talent, alongside the established classics that continue to fill the theatre.

Like all programme planners he had to tread the precarious path between full-length ballets and triple-bill evenings.

LEFT ABOVE Peter Darrell's 1979 production *Such Sweet Thunder* is a modern work in which he lined up Shakespeare's characters with top contemporary Hollywood personalities. Seen here is Telly Savalas (danced by Kenneth Saunders) as Julius Caesar, with his supporters (left to right), Fred Astaire, Gene Kelly, Donald O'Connor and James Cagney. They dance to the music of Duke Ellington. (*Scottish National Ballet, William Cooper*)

LEFT BELOW Members of the London Contemporary Dance Theatre performing Robert Cohan's ballet *Eos* in 1978. (*London Contemporary Dance Theatre, Anthony Crickmay*)

For the full-length ballet enthusiasts he produced reworked versions of *Giselle* and *Nutcracker*, and in 1979 he gave them an authentic Bournonville ballet *Napoli*. By way of contrast, that same season he produced his own ballet *Such Sweet Thunder* to the music of Duke Ellington. This set out to satirize Shakespeare by linking up his characters with Hollywood film and TV personalities. This convoluted train of thought ended up with Lady Macbeth appearing as Rita Hayworth, Oberon teamed up with Liberace, and Julius Caesar as Telly Savalas. Though the critics withheld their approval, it gave the dancers a lot of scope for mime and comedy, and the public enjoyed it.

In his years as director Peter Darrell not only achieved a solid following at home, but made his Scottish Ballet the first regional company to tour abroad.

The London Contemporary Dance Theatre, which is an offshoot of the Martha Graham company in America, concentrates entirely on modern dance. It owes its existence to a dedicated Martha Graham enthusiast Robin Howard, a Cambridge graduate who founded a school in 1966 to teach the Graham style. This grew into The London School of Contemporary Dance – the only one in Europe – and from this emerged the professional company of dancers known as The London Contemporary Dance Theatre. Robin Howard even bought London headquarters for them at The Place, next to St. Pancras' Church. Here he provided them with a small theatre studio for experimentation, as any member of the company has the right to try out ideas in the theatre workshop productions.

The artistic director Robert Cohan was Graham's partner and the company has maintained close links with its American parent. Their main concern, however, right from the start has been to develop their own choreographers. By 1974 these were beginning to emerge with Robert North and Siobhan Davies.

Although contemporary dance is a relative newcomer in Britain, it has developed strongly and attracts a sizeable following, especially among the younger generation. However, it remains to be seen whether contemporary and classical dance will contend with each other for supremacy or merge. For the present, both contribute to making Britain an important centre of the dance in the world today.

7

France, Belgium and Holland

The central creative force of ballet that passed from France to Russia in the days of the Tsars left the Paris Opéra in a state of mere survival. The only ballet of any importance to emerge was Saint-Léon's *Coppélia* in 1870.

Danced to an enchanting score by Délibes, the ballet tells the story of the old doll-maker Dr. Coppelius, whose masterpiece Coppélia is so life-like that a pair of young lovers, Franz and Swanilda, believe she is real and Franz falls in love with her. Swanilda, to get her own back on Franz and to fool Dr. Coppelius, pretends to be Coppélia. Eventually all the misunderstandings are sorted out and everyone is reconciled in a grand *divertissement*. In Paris the role of Franz was created by a ballerina, but when *Coppélia* travelled to St. Petersburg and became part of the Maryinsky repertoire, male dancers took over and it is this version by Petipa that most audiences see today.

The life of the Paris Opéra remained at a very low ebb all through the early years of the twentieth century. While Diaghilev's Ballets Russes took the city by storm, French dancers remained in the background, their morale undermined by the brilliance of the Russians and their opportunities frustrated by lack of great choreographers. Diaghilev's legacy to the French dancers, however, was his last star dancer Serge Lifar, who was to bring the Opéra back to life. Within weeks of Diaghilev's death in 1929 he had moved in as principal dancer and choreographer and before long he was also the artistic director.

Lifar was still only 24 years old with his whole career before him. He brought a surge of new vitality

Coppélia was the one great ballet to emerge in France during the last part of the nineteenth century. Created by choreographer Saint-Léon, it had its premiere in Paris in 1870, and has joined the ranks of the great popular classics. This contemporary production is by Roland Petit with Canadian ballerina Karen Kain in the leading role. (*Serge Lido*)

Serge Lifar, Diaghilev's last star dancer, became the leading dancer, choreographer and artistic director of the Paris Opéra. He is seen here in his own ballet *Icarus* in 1935. (*John Topham Picture Library*)

into the dusty corridors of the old theatre; the life of the Paris Opéra began to glow again, and Lifar himself was at the heart of it. His powerful stage presence and striking good looks could fill the theatre and most of his choreography was built round the Lifar image. It made life difficult for male dancers, but it presented splendid opportunities for the girls: Yvette Chauviré and Liane Daydé both came to the top at this time.

LEFT ABOVE In the famous *foyer* or lobby of the Paris Opéra in 1940, Serge Lifar beside the piano, rehearses one of the company's greatest dancers, Yvette Chauviré. (*Mansell Collection*)

LEFT BELOW *Les Forains* (The Street Players) 1945, was one of the first ballets produced by a young breakaway group from the Paris Opéra, who formed Les Ballets des Champs-Elysées. Seen here are Roland Petit, the choreographer, with Ludmila Tcherina. (*Serge Lido*)

RIGHT *Le Jeune Homme et la Mort* by Jean Cocteau with choreography by Roland Petit was produced by the Ballets des Champs-Elysées in 1946. Nathalie Philippart and Jean Babilée, seen here, created the leading roles. (*Serge Lido*)

When World War II plunged France into a struggle for survival under German occupation, Lifar remained faithfully at his post. Such is the human spirit that these were the years of his greatest creativity and one of his best-known surviving ballets is *Suite en Blanc* dating from 1943. It is one of the rare Lifar ballets that is pure dancing, a brilliant *divertissement* designed to show off classical dancers at their best.

When the war ended and divided France became mistress of her own destiny again, there was a witch hunt to flush out people who were thought to have collaborated with the Germans. The unfortunate Lifar was drawn into the net, and was banished from the Opéra in 1945. Since his ballets were also banned it left a serious gap in the repertoire and added to the general feeling of discontent that had been growing among the dancers.

Already some of the most promising and talented young dancers had left, among them 20-year-old Roland Petit with his partner Janine Charrat, the brilliant Jean Babilée and the exciting young dancer Renée Jeanmaire. They were joined by two men from Ballets Russes days, Boris Kochno, who had been Diaghilev's secretary and his old friend Jean Cocteau. Out of this group emerged a new company, Les Ballets des Champs-Elysées, the main creative force of which was Roland Petit, whose talents as a choreographer developed fast. They soon established themselves as the leading ballet group in France and one of their first productions to hit the headlines was Petit's, *Le Jeune Homme et la Mort* (1946). The story came from Cocteau and the music from Bach's *Passacaglia* in C minor.

The ballet tells of a young Parisian artist in his attic whose girl friend drives him to commit suicide, and he hangs himself; she returns with the mask of death to lead him away over the roof tops. The lights of the night-time city with the Eiffel tower and the flashing neon signs, created an emotive contrast to Bach's deeply moving music. The impact was tremendous, and it became a trend setter for post-war French ballet.

In spite of his success Roland Petit did not stay long with the company and in 1948 he formed his own Ballets de Paris with Renée Jeanmaire, whom he later married. Again it was success all the way for two years, one of the high spots being Petit's version of *Carmen* with Jeanmaire in the title role. After this they went to America to win fame and fortune in Hollywood films and revues, when Jeanmaire the ballerina became the star revue artist Zizi.

The Ballets des Champs-Elysées continued for another three years before folding up, its task completed. It had provided opportunities for a whole new generation of dancers.

In the meantime, Lifar, banished from Paris, had travelled south with Yvette Chauviré to join Le

Nouveau Ballet de Monte Carlo. This company had started in 1942 with dancers who had fled before the advancing German armies and pupils from local schools.

The year that Lifar and Chauviré joined them, the company was bought up by the wealthy Marquis de Cuevas from Chile, whose wife was a Rockefeller heiress. He turned it eventually into Le Grand Ballet du Marquis de Cuevas, an American orientated international touring company, relying on big names and established ballets for its box office appeal. Though it provided a platform for many talented dancers it never managed any creative contributions and remained a rich man's hobby. After the death of the Marquis in 1961 the company disbanded.

Carmen has been one of Roland Petit's most successful ballets. First produced in 1949 for his own new company, Ballet de Paris, he is seen here in the leading role, with his wife Zizi Jeanmaire. (*Serge Lido*)

RIGHT *Nijinsky, Clown de Dieu* is Béjart's ballet on the life of Nijinsky, produced in 1971. American Suzanne Farrell, top ballerina of the company at the time, dances the role of Nijinsky's ideal, with Jorge Donn as Nijinsky himself. (*Mike Davis Studios, Jesse Davis*)

Lifar spent two years in exile before the clamour of his dancers at the Opéra persuaded the management to have him back. He returned in 1947 as choreographer only, although later he was also allowed to appear on stage again. Though he was happy to be back and worked on a series of ballets, things were never quite the same again and, in 1958, he finally left to pursue the life of a freelance artist.

Once more the Opéra was left without a strong guiding hand. A number of directors came and went and for years the company appeared to be drifting. It was only after Rolf Liebermann arrived from Hamburg in 1973 to take over as director, that things began to happen. He quickly shaped a new policy: the classical repertoire was enriched by works from Balanchine, Béjart and Petit, a modern dance section of the company was formed and he even commissioned a full-length work from avant-garde Merce Cunningham. So, the old Opéra was brought once more into the contemporary mainstream.

By this time Roland Petit and Renée Jeanmaire were back in Paris where they bought the Casino de Paris in 1970 and used it to stage revues for Zizi. Since 1972 Petit has directed the Ballet de Marseille, attracting many of the best dancers, writers and artists for his productions. Critics have accused him of being a choreographic lightweight, but the public happily continues to flock to his ballets and enjoy his special blend of brilliance, chic and superb sense of theatre that is uniquely French.

The Russian dancers left in France after Diaghilev's death went through years of great change and upheaval. Two companies started up almost immediately: Les Ballets de l'Opéra de Monte Carlo, managed by Frenchman René Blum, and Le Ballet de l'Opéra Russe à Paris, directed by Colonel de Basil who was said to have been a Cossack general. The two merged in 1932 to become Les Ballets Russes de Monte Carlo.

This time it seemed everything was going right for them. Colonel de Basil was the organizing, business brain; René Blum, the man of culture, was the artistic director. They had the faithful Grigoriev, who had been Diaghilev's stage manager for twenty years, and they had the great choreographers, Balanchine, Massine, Fokine and Nijinska. They

Béjart has taken his company all over the world. Here Jorge Donn is dancing in *Amor de Poeta* in the Colón Theatre in Buenos Aires. (*Jorge Fama*)

CENTRE *Le Sacre du Printemps*, Nijinsky's ballet, ahead of its time in 1913, received a new lease of life in 1959 when Maurice Béjart presented his version of it in Brussels. Its success led to the launching of his company, The Ballet of the 20th Century. Suzanne Farrell is seen here in a more recent production. (*Mike Davis Studios, Jesse Davis*)

RIGHT *Notre Faust* is another Béjart ballet, first produced in 1975. Béjart himself is seen here in the part of Faust. (*Serge Lido*)

also had their pick of the best young talent coming out of the schools of the old Russian dancers who had settled in France, which gave them the famous 'baby ballerinas': 13-year-old Baronova, 14-year-old Toumanova, and 15-year-old Riabouchinska, as well as David Lichine from the Ida Rubinstein company.

To start with it was success all the way. They toured Europe, had a triumph in London and went off to the United States under the management of impressario Sol Hurok. It seemed like the great old days again, but it needed a Diaghilev to hold things together. Blum and de Basil were uneasy colleagues and finally they quarrelled and the company split apart in a welter of ill feeling. By 1936 there were two rival companies once more.

Blum continued to do the Monte Carlo season and toured Europe, but the war brought tragedy, for when the Germans occupied France he was deported to the concentration camp at Auschwitz and died there in 1944. Blum's death broke the last links with Monte Carlo. The company moved out to America where it was managed for a time by Hurok, and then formed into a non-profit making concern doing occasional tours until it faded away in 1962.

The de Basil company, that had set off for Australia and America during the war, were also managed for a time by Hurok. They toured extensively in both North and South America, finally settling in Buenos Aires. De Basil died in 1951 and though Grigoriev and his wife tried to revive the company, it disbanded the following year.

So, the last of the great Diaghilev heritage was left scattered across the Americas.

BELGIUM

In Belgium the ballet scene is dominated by one name, Béjart and his Ballet of the 20th Century, which came into existence in 1960 and is based on the Théâtre Royal de la Monnaie in Brussels.

Actually, this historic theatre, first built in 1705, has a long association with ballet. In the nineteenth century the great name of Petipa was associated with it: Jean Petipa was ballet master at intervals between 1819 and 1843 and founded the Conservatoire de la Danse, and here his two famous sons Lucien and Marius made their débuts. He also put the city on the touring map by inviting all the great ballerinas of the day to make guest appearances. Lucien returned in 1872 as ballet master, but unfortunately for Belgium he lacked his brother's choreographic genius, and by the turn of the century ballet was wilting. It did not really revive again until Béjart appeared on the scene.

Maurice Béjart, like Marius Petipa, was born in Marseilles, but unlike Marius, the son of a dancer, Maurice was the surprising offspring of a philosopher. He trained as a dancer in the Russian tradition, with Egorova in Paris and Volkova in London, and went on to a mixed experience with various classical and modern companies. This thrusting, intelligent, highly individual young man lost no time, however, in forming a company of his own, and proceeded to make it known by a series of original works that he produced for Belgian television.

This led to a commission from the director of the Théâtre de la Monnaie for a new ballet. What he got in 1959 was Béjart's powerful version of the old *Sacre du Printemps*. The result was spectacular and it was awarded 'Le Prix de l'Université de la Danse'. As a result, the company, that had been specially assembled to dance the ballet, became the nucleus of the Ballet of the 20th Century, which Béjart continues to direct.

Béjart is a man who thinks big: he uses the music of big names like Beethoven and Wagner; he

Maria Koppers, a fine classical dancer, in the leading role in the Dutch National Ballet's production of *The Firebird*. (*Mike Davis Studios, Jesse Davis*)

mounts big spectacles in all kinds of unconventional places and attracts huge audiences of enthusiastic young people. Older ballet-goers and critics find him controversial for he is incessantly exploring. His experiments have ranged from pure dance, in his exciting *Boléro* with Ravel's music, to total spectacle with singing and poetry in *Tales of Hoffmann*, as well as dramatic ballet and interpretations of great

LEFT The Ballet of the 20th Century has assembled a high-powered collection of international talent, including Maina Gielgud, niece of Sir John, seen here with leading Italian dancer Paolo Bortoluzzi. (*Mike Davis Studios, Jesse Davis*)

orchestral music such as Beethoven's *Ninth Symphony*. His exploration into far eastern religion produced his own brand of mystic ballet in *Nijinksy, Clown de Dieu* (1971) which deals with Nijinksy's inner tensions between his love for his art, his links with Diaghilev, his love for the woman he sees as his ideal, and his vision of God.

Inevitably, also, with such an avant-garde innovation, there has been as assortment of scandalous ballets such as *Erotica* and *Variations pour une Porte et un Soupir* about man-eating females, in which Béjart created a solo role for Maina Gielgud.

Béjart's dancers have come from a wide variety of countries; among them have been soloist Jorge Donn from the Argentine and Paolo Bortoluzzi, one of the finest Italian dancers today, who went on to join the American Theater Ballet. Though other choreographers have contributed to the repertoire and young dancers are encouraged to experiment themselves, it is still Béjart, the man of the theatre, who remains the vital force behind this company.

Antwerp also has a company of its own, The Ballet of Flanders, started in 1969 and which now has about fifty dancers in a mixed repertoire.

HOLLAND

Although it is usually said that Holland's ballet history began less than fifty years ago, Amsterdam saw its first ballet over three hundred years ago in 1642 when *The Ballet of the Five Senses* was staged in its recently opened theatre. All through the nineteenth century ballet activity continued, mostly in the capable hands of Andries van Hamme and his son Anton, who were ballet masters of the Amsterdam Theatre and built up a company of about sixty dancers. The Dutch were also so much ahead of the times that they allowed female dancers on stage long before they were seen in Paris.

It was only at the turn of the century that ballet

The Netherlands Dance Theatre in *Mutations*, a work by Glen Tetley and van Manen, first produced in 1970. The ballet combines live dance and film and parts of it are danced in the nude. (*Mike Davis Studios, Jesse Davis*)

seemed to lose its way and the company was reduced to the role of poor relation to the opera. Even Pavlova could not revive it and, almost symbolically it would seem, she herself died in Holland in 1931.

When the first spark of renewed life came it was not with classical ballet but modern dance.

German-born Yvonne Georgi and her partner Harald Kreutzberg came to Amsterdam to give recitals in the 1930s. They belonged to the Dalcroze-Wigman-Jooss school, and their style of dancing generated so much enthusiasm that Georgi formed a company in Holland.

World War II put everything into abeyance, but from 1946 onwards there was an explosion of activity. Theatres opened again, the company in Amsterdam was re-formed and one of Georgi's soloists Mascha Weeme even started a company of her own. Then, on this modern dance scene arrived a classical Russian dancer Sonia Gaskell, who had been teaching in Paris, and she started a ballet recital group that grew into Het Nederlands Ballet. Surprisingly enough, classical and modern merged; Gaskell and Weeme came together and, in 1961, the Dutch National Ballet was created.

Today it has grown into a full-sized company with an impressive repertoire of Russian classics and modern works. Its creative impulsion comes from three highly talented men: Rudi van Dantzig, who is now artistic director, choreographer Hans van Manen and the versatile Toer van Schayk, who is dancer, choreographer and, above all, artist – he does most of the décors for his colleague's ballets. All three had a classical foundation, having danced with Sonia Gaskell, and all three developed a highly effective and original blend of classical and modern in their work.

Dantzig ballets are mainly concerned with the problems of people. One of the first that launched him to success was his *Monument for a Dead Boy* in 1965. This shows, in a series of flashbacks, the life of a homosexual boy pursuing an inner artistic vision that draws him into ever greater isolation and finally destroys him.

Van Manen is more concerned with form and music. He also likes to introduce an element of surprise, which he did recently in the 1979 Holland Festival with his new ballet *Live*, a reference to live television. A startled audience saw two dancers and a man in black leather with a video camera. Most of the action was focussed on the girl dancer's solos; as she moved to the music of Liszt the audience, watching her live, saw her at the same time through the camera, projected from totally different angles onto an outsize television screen stretched across the back of the stage. This was not a gimmick. This was van Manen using video as a tool to explore the innovatory idea of looking at the same movement in three dimensions, and mixing past and present. Such was his artistry that it was extraordinarily effective and could well open up new prospects for choreographers to explore.

Pure modern dance flourishes in Holland in the Netherlands Dance Theatre, based on the Hague. This was a breakaway group started in 1959 by American Benjamin Harkarvy, who had been Gaskell's ballet master. Van Dantzig and van Manen helped to get the company established, and it was further strengthened by two more powerful young choreographers in the same idiom: Glen Tetley from America and their own Jaap Flier. The result has been a very special style of dancing that cannot be labelled classical, Wigman or Graham, but is very much the company's own and has established a solid international reputation for the Netherlands Dance Theatre.

To complete the picture, the dancers of tomorrow are catered for in Amsterdam by the Scapino Ballet, which mounts programmes for children and was, in fact, the first company to get going after the war.

Holland has come a very long way in a very short time, and now ranks among the leading dance centres of the world.

8

United States, Canada and Cuba

The development of the dance in the United States is woven in a fascinating pattern because of the many vivid threads that have gone into its formation.

America, like Russia, had a strong tradition of folk dancing, but of a much wider variety for it was brought by settlers from many different cultures. As in Russia, this grass-roots dancing came into contact with the imported ideas of European ballet. Unlike Tsarist Russia, however, free America could accept or reject the new ideas, and in true democratic style did both. Opinions were divided, and the result has been the development side by side of two powerful dance idioms – classical ballet and modern dance.

The story goes that modern dance was born on a day long ago in the 1880s, when young Isadora Duncan kicked off her ballet shoes and danced barefoot; the great challenge to classical ballet had begun. Isadora's début in Chicago in 1899 was a failure, so she set out to conquer Europe: a bare-foot Joan of Arc, waving the banner of free-style dancing.

Meanwhile, another pioneer was growing up. Ruth St Denis had not been trained in classical ballet, she had learned social dancing and mime from her mother and made her début in a New York music hall. She branched off when she became fascinated by exotic dancing and started composing her own Hindu-style dances at a time when the wave of enthusiasm for things exotic was just beginning. These dances carried her to success on a triumphant three-year tour of Europe and, back home again, she went from strength to strength with big American tours. In 1914 she met a young dancer Ted Shawn, whom she married in August that same year. She was by now 37 years old and well established, he was 24 and just starting. His training had been on classical lines, and he was on his first tour with a small company that had developed from his school in Los Angeles.

Classical ballet and exotic free-style dancing merged. They became dancing partners, and to-gether set up their famous Denishawn school in Los Angeles, with a touring company. The school became the launching pad for the leaders of modern American dancing: Martha Graham, Doris Humphrey and Charles Weidman.

These youngsters of the 1920s, belonging to the scientific age, had more sophisticated ideas than their teachers and became interested in applying scientific principles to the idea of expressing feeling through movement. Doris Humphrey and Charles Weidman set up their own school in 1927, and the technique they evolved was known as 'fall and recovery'.

Briefly, the idea is that dance, representing movement and life, exists as an arc between two static states representing death: horizontal death, when the body lies flat on the ground, and vertical death, when it is standing erect and motionless. If the body moves from the vertical, gravity pulls it down; while if it moves from the horizontal, the body's own efforts against gravity, make it recover. This 'fall and recovery' also symbolizes man's two-fold longing for security and his urge to explore the unknown.

These ideas were developed in the dances Humphrey and Weidman created, such as *Water Study* (1928) inspired by nature; the abstract *Drama of Motion* (1931) and the *New Dance* (1935), an epic series envisaging an ideal world in which each individual is self-fulfilled in a harmonious relationship with others. Comedy played no part in this world, nor did theatrical spectacle and dramatic virtuosity. Their sole concern was communication through movement, and their ideas and technique had a profound influence on their contemporaries.

While Humphrey and Weidman were to become

The Owl and the Pussycat by the Martha Graham company, with Yuriko Kimura and Tim Wengerd as leading dancers and Liza Minelli as the narrator, had its London premiere at Covent Garden in 1979. (*Mike Davis Studios, Jesse Davis*)

114

household names in America, Martha Graham was to go beyond this to achieve world fame. She emerged from Denishawn in 1923, by which time she was 29 years old. Her late start was due to her father, who was bitterly opposed to her desire to dance. Ten generations of American history had gone into this passionate, dynamic woman, whose life was to span nearly a century. Scottish, Irish and Dutch strains were woven into her genetic inheritance, along with a strong thread of religious puritanism, and all of these were reflected in her many dance creations. There was nothing in her

Ruth St. Denis and her husband Ted Shawn in one of their exotic, free-style dances. (*Mansell Collection*)

RIGHT Martha Graham brought the art and technique of contemporary dance to new high standards, and has had a powerful influence on the development of modern dance. She is seen here in *Clytemnestra*, a dramatic ballet based on three Greek tragedies by Aeschylus. (*Mike Davis Studios, Jesse Davis*)

immediate background, however, to suggest the explosive genius that was to emerge, for her father was a physician and her mother had no connection with the theatre.

Martha spent seven years at Denishawn, training in the school and dancing with the company. As a dancer she rapidly made herself noticed by her strong dramatic qualities and her magnetic stage presence, and before long had outgrown her teachers, although it took several agonizing years for her own distinctive genius to emerge. It was not until 1930 that she had fully worked out her ideas of how to use the body to express an emotion without relying on narrative or mime.

There were two main principles: first that the source of all movement is in the back. From the impulsion in the back come the movements of the arms and legs. (This is why Graham classes mostly start lying on the floor). The second principle is that of 'contraction and release'. This is centred on breathing, the basic human life movement which contracts and releases muscles for our vital air supply. This is not only a physical fact, but is at the heart of many mystic religious practices such as yoga. On these foundations Martha Graham built a whole grammar of movement capable of being taught.

Her first dance creations centred around the figure of the American woman: she was the bride in *Appalachian Spring* (1944). But the range extended to other characters such as the Brontë sisters in *Deaths and Entrances*, and in due course she explored Greek mythology which resulted in works like *Cave of the Heart* (1946) and *Night Journey* (1947) that showed the heroine reliving her past life. She also went into history and presented great women, such as Joan of Arc in *Seraphic Dialogue* (1955).

By this time the world had accepted what Martha Graham had to say. She could relax and even look at classical ballet. Some movements from the enemy camp began to infiltrate the Graham severity, producing more lyrical and flowing lines. She extended her technique to introduce male dancers to her original all-female company and, even more surprising, a sense of humour began to lighten the solemnity of the dance.

When the Graham company appeared in London's Covent Garden in 1979, they presented the British premiere of *The Owl and the Pussy Cat*. Though it was solemnly billed as, 'The eternal question of relationships and a voyage', the more superficial theatre-goer could enjoy it as a delightful and amusing presentation of Hilaire Belloc's poem,

Merce Cunningham was a pupil of Martha Graham and danced in her company. He broke away, forming his own group in 1952; since then he has experimented along his own lines with pure movement and pure sound. He has made an important contribution to the art of contemporary dance. (*Mike Davis Studios, Jesse Davis*)

spoken by Liza Minelli, with a brilliantly witty performance by Yuriko Kimura as the pussy cat.

By this time, Martha Graham, now aged 85, had at last admitted defeat and given up dancing herself, though she continued to travel with her company and was still the power behind the scenes.

It was probably as a revolt against the overwhelming Graham personality that one of her pupils Merce Cunningham broke away in 1945, after six years with her group, and went on to form his own company in 1952, collaborating with composer John Cage. Cunningham discarded the Graham belief that an artist has a right to impose his own personality on an audience, or that choreography could be a means of projecting one's personality. John Cage, in his own field, discarded the traditional harmony and structure of western style music. Together Cunningham and Cage experimented endlessly; Cunningham with pure movement, Cage with pure sound, often produced electronically.

Cunningham, explaining his theories to a British television audience in 1979 told them:

'*Dancing for me is movement in time and space. Dances are intended to be the activities of humans moving in different ways. We have chosen to have the music and the dance as separate identities. It is meant as an opening out into the complexity we live in.*'

One of the best-known results of this philosophy of the dance is *The Rain Forest*, with electronic sounds and a décor by Andy Warhol.

Merce Cunningham's ideas have a host of followers, and the contemporary dance is very active in America. Among the leaders of today's avant-garde movement are Twyla Tharp and Paul Taylor, while in San Francisco Anne Halprin's dancers' workshop continues to be a great centre for dance happenings.

Classical ballet did not put down serious roots in America until well into the 1930s, but has been making up for the late start by the speed and range of its development. Classical dancing had, of course, been seen regularly in the big cities as improved travelling conditions brought visitors from Europe, such as Fanny Elssler in 1840, the Petipa family about the same time, and Léon Espinosa who was nearly captured by Indians.

It was not all one way traffic however, for America produced a home-grown ballerina of its own, the first to be exported to Europe. Augusta Maywood, born in New York in 1825, had trained in Philadelphia and made her début there in 1837 in *Le Dieu et la Bayadère*. This ballet was an earlier version of Petipa's *La Bayadère*, and both were based on a ballad by the German poet Goethe. The earlier version had had its premiere in Paris in 1830 with Marie Taglioni in the role of Zoloé, a role specially choreographed for her by her father.

It was to Paris that Augusta Maywood travelled, to continue studying at the Opéra. She went on to Vienna and Milan, where she appeared at La Scala sharing ballerina roles with Fanny Elssler.

By the beginning of the twentieth century, American audiences were welcoming such stars as Adeline Genée, Pavlova, and the great dancers of the Ballets Russes. All these, however, were birds of passage, and the Americans did not get seriously involved in the art until the 1920s when the aftermath of the Russian revolution and the subsequent break up of Diaghilev's Ballets Russes scattered dancers and choreographers across the world, many of whom came to settle in the United States.

One of the first to arrive was Fokine, who came in 1923 and made New York his home until he died in 1942. Adolph Bolm arrived with the Ballets Russes and stayed to work in New York and Chicago, finally opening a school in San Francisco. In 1924 Pavlova's partner Mordkin settled in the States to become one of the founding fathers of American ballet. Teaching in New York and Philadelphia, he formed his own company in 1937 to display his pupils' talents – among them Judy Garland and Nijinsky's daughter Kyra. Out of this grew the great American Ballet Theater company.

It was formed in 1939 as the Ballet Theater ('American' was added later) and gave its first professional performance on 1 January 1940 in New York. The driving force behind the venture was the company's ballerina Lucia Chase with Mordkin's theatre agent Richard Pleasant. It was thanks to Lucia Chase, who used her personal fortune to back the company, that it was able to get started and for thirty years she devoted her energies and money to help keep it going.

The company's policy was fairly amorphous. The general idea was to produce the best of the classics and build up an American repertoire alongside them. Inevitably they started off dominated by the great pre-war Ballets Russes: Fokine staged *Les Sylphides* and *Carnaval* for them; Anton Dolin produced *Giselle* and *Swan Lake* in which he and Markova danced; Adolph Bolm produced a highly successful version of *Peter and the Wolf*, and Massine spent two years with them, creating his gipsy ballet *Aleko* in 1942 and *Mam'zelle Angot* in 1943.

It was not long, however, before a new generation was making its presence felt. From London's Ballet Rambert came Antony Tudor and Andrée Howard with leading dancer Hugh Laing. Soon

Paul Taylor danced with Martha Graham and the Cunningham companies, and has gone on to become one of the leading contemporary choreographers in the world of modern dance, producing imaginative and often humourous ballets. (*Mike Davis Studios, Jesse Davis*)

Fancy Free, Jerome Robbins's first ballet, was such a success that it was turned into the Broadway hit musical *On The Town*. This picture is from the original production by the American Ballet Theater in 1944. (*Mander & Mitchenson Theatre Collection*)

after arrived American-born, Rambert-trained Agnes de Mille, who had been touring Europe until the outbreak of war. This niece of the film magnate Cecil B de Mille, started her choreographic career with American Ballet Theater. She produced her first important work *Black Ritual* for them in 1940, followed by several more ballets before she moved to Broadway to create the dances in the musicals *Oklahoma* and *Carousel*.

New York-born Jerome Robbins moved in the opposite direction, for he came off Broadway in 1940 to join the American Ballet Theater as a dancer after an encyclopaedic training as a dancer and a musician. His first ballet for the company was

Fancy Free in 1944, to Bernstein's score. It was such a sensational success that he and Bernstein translated it into commercial theatre terms and it became the Broadway musical hit *On the Town*. This launched Robbins on a two-way choreographic career as he continued to produce ballets while going on to world-wide success in such shows as *West Side Story*, *The King and I* and *Fiddler on the Roof*.

As far as American Ballet Theater was concerned, Robbins and Tudor were the two most powerful influences in the formative years. They remained with the company long enough to build up its repertoire and to create their own special kind of dancer, such as Rosella Hightower, who was their soloist in the 1940s. A dancer of dazzling technique, she went on to become the leading ballerina in the Grand Ballet du Marquis de Cuevas.

There were the sisters, Maria and Marjorie Tall-chief who were of Red Indian descent and brought the grace and strength of their ancestry to a beautiful classical line. Maria went on to become the leading ballerina with the New York City Ballet and married Balanchine, while Marjorie, after two years with ABT, went on to Paris to become the first American star dancer at the Opéra.

There was also a brilliant trio of dancers from Cuba, the brothers Alberto and Fernando Alonso, with Fernando's wife Alicia, whose story belongs to the National Ballet of Cuba.

This rapid turnover of dancers was always American Ballet Theater's big problem as it prevented them from establishing a real identity. They did, however, collect an impressive list of guest

stars – among them the great French dancer Jean Babilée the Russian Nureyev, and Natalia Makarova from the Kirov ballet who chose life in the west in 1970. Baryshnikov, another of the great stars of the Kirov, who asked for asylum in Canada in 1974, danced regularly for American Ballet Theater before joining the New York City Ballet. He returned, however, in 1980 as their artistic director and his influence could mean the opening of a new chapter in the company's history.

In 1979 the first defector from Moscow's Bolshoi ballet Alexander Godunov, left during an American tour and joined the American Ballet Theater. He was followed a few days later by his colleagues Leonid Koslov and his wife Valentina, both talented young dancers with promising futures ahead of them.

Rosella Hightower as the Queen Butterfly in *Piège de Lumière* (*The Light Trap*) produced by the Marquis de Cuevas's Ballet in 1952. (*John Topham Picture Library*)

Patricia McBride became New York City Ballet's youngest principal dancer in 1961. She has created an impressive list of parts in both Balanchine and Robbins ballets and is seen here in Robbins's *Other Dances*. Jean-Pierre Bonnefous is also a leading dancer with the company. (*Mike Davis Studios, Jesse Davis*)

OPPOSITE *Square Dance* is a Balanchine ballet created for the New York City ballet in 1957. The dancers in this recent production are Merrill Ashley and Sean Lavery. (*Mike Davis Studios, Jesse Davis*)

RIGHT *Symphony in C,* another Balanchine ballet originally known as *Palais de Cristal*, was renamed in 1948. Danced to music by Bizet, it is a plotless ballet designed to show off the talents of the dancers. In this recent production they are Suzanne Farrell and Peter Martins, two of New York City Ballet's top performers. (*Mike Davis Studios, Jesse Davis*)

In sharp contrast to American Ballet Theater with its wide range of choreographers, New York City Ballet grew up round the talent of one man, George Balanchine and it had a gestation period of fourteen years! The original idea came from writer

122

Maria Tallchief in the New York City Ballet's production of *Swan Lake*, partnered by André Prokovsky. (*Martha Swope*)

Lincoln Kirstein, who wanted to see a truly American style of classical dancing established. He made a start in 1933 by inviting Balanchine to New York to set up a ballet school to train dancers for a future company. The School of American Ballet was established in 1935, but the rest of the project was brutally interrupted by World War II and it was not until 1946 that they were able to get going again.

Balanchine formed the Ballet Society, a self-financing venture, that not only survived but flourished and became an artistic force to be reckoned with. It received its name New York City Ballet in 1948 and the following year Jerome Robbins joined as assistant director.

The Balanchine-Robbins choreography became the hallmark of the New York City Ballet and the school evolved a special type of Balanchine female dancer. She is lean and long-limbed, with the speed of a racehorse and a great strength of leg – the reverse, in fact, of the old image of the compact, softly contoured ballerina, whose main attraction lay in the fluidity and grace of her arm movements.

For Balanchine dancing and music are the most important ingredients of ballet, story line and décor are secondary. This is why so many Balanchine ballets are danced in practice clothes, with a deadpan expression, on a bare stage. He has always seemed at his happiest working with his old friend Stravinsky to produce such ballets as *Variations* (1966), *Violin Concerto* and *Duo Concertant*, both in 1972.

His output, however, has been enormous and

wide ranging. He has produced his own versions of the classics such as *Swan Lake* and *Nutcracker*, while his versatility is such that he has ranged from the romantic *Serenade* to dramatic subjects like *The Prodigal Son*, and avant-garde works like *Agon* and *The Four Temperaments*, which deals in an abstract manner with the classic moods of man: 'melancholic', 'sanguine', 'phlegmatic' and 'choleric'.

When New York City Ballet came to London in 1979 on their first visit for fourteen years, British audiences had the rare opportunity of seeing top American dancers, Pat McBride, Suzanne Farrell and Merrill Ashley with Sean Lavery and Robert

Baryshnikov, former star of the Kirov Ballet, became Director of the American Ballet Theater in 1980. He is seen here in *Giselle* partnering Makarova, who left the Kirov company in 1970. (*Mike Davis Studios, Jesse Davis*)

Weiss, in a massive repertoire of thirty ballets.

Only a month before, in August that same year, London audiences had also displayed tremendous enthusiasm for another visiting American company, The Dance Theater of Harlem, which came to the Sadler's Wells Theatre.

This all-black company of classical dancers had been started less than ten years earlier by Arthur Mitchell, a black dancer with the New York City Ballet. A fine performer himself and a man of enormous courage and vision, he wanted to do something for his own people. He started in his own home ground in Harlem, where he was born, by giving lessons in classical ballet in an old garage. The response was overwhelming; in no time at all his original class of thirty had grown to over four-hundred. Helped and encouraged by Balanchine and Robbins, a company was formed that made its

début in 1971. Three years later it was giving a New York season and touring the States, since then it has never looked back.

Under Arthur Mitchell's brilliant direction and firm discipline, these highly trained dancers have brought to classical ballet their own brand of vitality and innate joy in movement which have created their own completely individual style. They have the temperament and the skill to range happily and successfully from noble, graceful classical roles, which they invest with tremendous dignity, to comedy, drama and exhilarating African jazz idioms. In a ballet like *Mirage (The Games People Play)* they combine the two, as it portrays contrasting groups of people – the elegant and the beautifully dressed, moving with classic grace, against the Crazies, in their violent red clothes. For black dancers, movement is life and dancing is their special language. It looks as though they have a great deal to say to the rest of the world.

Two dancers from the all-black company The Dance Theater of Harlem in *Combat*. They demonstrate the vitality and technical virtuosity for which the company is famous. (*Mike Davis Studios, Jesse Davis*)

LEFT The Dance Theater of Harlem in *Mirage (The Games People Play)* with Darrell Davis, Mel Tomlinson, Stephanie Baxter and Karen Brown. (*Mike Davis Studios, Jesse Davis*)

Though the three main companies in America are New York-based, regional companies have proliferated all over the States. The National Association of Regional Ballets has helped and encouraged many groups to get started, often with generous subsidies from commercial sources: the Ford Foundation alone made a grant of over seven million dollars in 1973. So, the young American dancers and choreographers of today are being given their opportunity to create the American ballet of tomorrow.

CANADA

Across the border in Canada, ballet has also put down vigorous roots, though the original impetus came mostly from Britain.

One of the first companies was the Royal Winnipeg Ballet that started life in 1939 as an amateur ballet club, founded by Lancashire-born Gweneth Lloyd. It grew to professional status and achieved another 'first' when it was granted the royal charter by Queen Elizabeth II in 1953.

In Toronto the National Ballet of Canada got under way in 1951. It was one of Ninette de Valois's dancers Celia Franca, who founded the company and spent the next twenty years working to establish it. She brought to Canadian dancers the legacy of her own training under Tudor and Idzikowsky, and her experience with the Ballet Rambert and Sadler's Wells Ballet. British-born Betty Oliphant joined her in 1959 to found the National Ballet school which she continued to run until 1979.

Celia Franca always insisted that the classics are the basis of any ballet repertoire and she worked unremittingly to build up this side of the company's achievement, facing the sniping from nationalists who accused her of trying to make another British Royal Ballet on Canadian soil. It was, however, her policy also to produce contemporary Canadian works and she started a theatre workshop to encourage young talent.

This side of the company's activities has been further developed by Alexander Grant since he took over as artistic director in 1976.

In Alexander Grant the Canadians have a New Zealander whose dancing career had been exclusively with the Royal Ballet, but who has since channelled his exuberant vitality and enthusiasm into the Canadian ballet scene. He has given his

George Balanchine and Jerome Robbins at work in the rehearsal studio of the New York City Ballet. (*Martha Swope*)

129

LEFT The National Ballet of Canada in *Kettentanz*, a chain of dances for six couples to polkas, galops and waltzes by Richard Strauss. (*Mike Davis Studios, Jesse Davis*)

BELOW Karen Kain, born in 1951, was trained in the Canadian National Ballet School and joined the company in 1969. She has since become one of their top dancers, and has achieved an international reputation as a guest artist and by her television appearances. Here she is seen in *Giselle*. (*Mike Davis Studios, Jesse Davis*)

young choreographers a boost by putting some of their workshop try-outs into the company's main repertoire; a bold move as it meant taking big box office risks, especially in Canada where ballet-goers tend to be conservative in their tastes.

It did, however, give audiences in Toronto and New York the chance to see such works as Anne Ditchburn's *Mad Shadows* – one of her most successful creations that was later taken up by the film

Europe. Her frequent film and television appearances have also won her a wide public following. In 1979 the British public had the chance of seeing her when the National Ballet of Canada gave a summer season at Covent Garden.

CUBA

That same summer of 1979, British ballet-goers had a feast of dancing from the new world. In three event-packed months, London audiences saw the Martha Graham company, the New York City Ballet and the Harlem Dance Theater, as well as the National Ballet of Canada. Then, as an added bonus, there was a first-time-ever visit from the

Celia Franca, founder of the National Ballet of Canada, is seen here as a dancer with the Sadler's Wells Ballet in London in 1942. She is the Queen (*right*) with Robert Helpmann as Hamlet and Margot Fonteyn as Ophelia. (*London, Royal Opera House Archives*)

world; James Kudelka's *Washington Square*, based on the Henry James novel and Greek-born Constantin Patsalas's version of the *Rite of Spring*, which aroused a lot of interest as it bore the hallmarks of a highly individual talent to be watched.

Appearances by guest stars have been a great help and inspiration to this company, especially the continuing visits of Rudolf Nureyev and the great Danish dancer Erik Bruhn. More recently, his fellow Dane Peter Schaufuss joined the company as principal dancer, before going on to a freelance life. Among their top ballerinas is Ontario-born Karen Kain whose technique and artistry have won her an international reputation. She was Nureyev's regular partner in Canada and has toured with him in

National Ballet of Cuba, who came to the Edinburgh Festival where a lucky first night audience saw the legendary Alicia Alonso dancing *Giselle* with her company. Alicia has been ranked among the finest Giselle's of the century and, although she was 62 years old, her artistry still won the hearts of her public and the critics.

The story of this frail looking romantic ballerina is one of incredible toughness and courage. Alicia Martinez was born in Havana in 1917 – the same year that the indefatigable Pavlova and her company arrived to bring the Cubans one of their rare glimpses of classical ballet. Alicia went to study ballet in New York where she met fellow Cuban Fernando Alonso, who was studying with Mordkin.

Alicia Alonso, founder of the National Ballet of Cuba, in the rehearsal studio with Josefina Mendez, *prima ballerina* of the company. (*Edinburgh International Festival*)

LEFT New Zealander, Alexander Grant has been the artistic director of Canada's National Ballet since 1976. He is seen here in his early days as a dancer with the Royal Ballet, partnering Merle Park in the tango from *Façade*. (*London, Royal Opera House Archives*)

She married him when she was 16, and they went on to join the American Ballet Theater.

Though they were seeking personal fame and fortune, they never lost their strong ties of loyalty to their own country and dreamed of one day establishing a national ballet in Cuba. They would go back to their country whenever they could to spend their time and money teaching and producing shows. In 1955 they managed to form the Ballet de Cuba, which struggled on until the turning point came with the arrival in 1959 of Fidel Castro, who quickly recognized the value of their contribution to

133

The National Ballet of Cuba at the Edinburgh Festival in 1979 with Alicia Alonso dancing *Giselle*. This has always been acclaimed as one of her greatest roles. (*Edinburgh International Festival*)

Cuba's cultural life. Suddenly, the struggling company, now called the National Ballet of Cuba, found itself installed in the spacious surroundings of an ex-country club, and here Fernando had the opportunity to develop his astonishing gifts as a teacher.

Alicia herself developed as a choreographer while continuing to dance. Few people realized that through all these years this indomitable woman had had to fight the personal tragedy of near-blindness. Two detached retinas almost destroyed her sight: on stage she was totally dependant on her partner to know where she was. Off stage she could only work using powerful binoculars, which may well account for the precision and attention to detail that is a hallmark of her productions. It was only many years later that an operation on her eyes was successful and restored much of her sight.

Together the Alonsos brought their company to such a high professional standard that they were able to tour the communist circuit of China, Russia and Eastern Europe, while their individual dancers became formidable medal winners both in Moscow and in the international Varna competitions.

Cuban ballet has been a fascinating growth for, once again, classical technique has been grafted onto a vigorous young rootstock. In Cuba this was a blend of Spanish and African tradition, full of fire, vitality and proud dignity. It had already given rise to the Rumba!

As an interesting example of ballet genetics, Alicia's brother-in-law Alberto Alonso, with a fine classical Russian ballet heritage, married one of the great Cuban rumba dancers Simone Allero. The result in her performances was a sensational presentation of classical rumba, that cannot fail to influence future dancers.

It is this blend of genes that has given the National Ballet of Cuba its highly individual identity and continues to revitalize classical ballet in that country.

9

Russia

The tide of revolution that swept away the Tsars in 1917 came dangerously close to sweeping away their two Imperial theatres also.

'Down with ballet', was the cry, following the revolutionary reasoning that, because it was associated with the hated Tsars, it was therefore no good for the masses. What people wanted was a new sort of dancing to express modern life. So said the extremists. As it turned out they were wrong. The masses did not really like the modern experimental dances that were served up to them during the 1920s. They preferred *Swan Lake*, and it was thanks

The Kirov Ballet in their production of *Sleeping Beauty*.
(*Mike Davis Studios, Jesse Davis*)

to the dedicated loyalty of a handful of teachers that *Swan Lake* and its classical contemporaries continued to exist.

The Soviets came, in the end, to be very proud of their heritage. The battle, however, went on for about ten years before it was finally realized that the classical ballet system knew better than any other how to train the human body, and that what was needed was not a new form of dance, but new outlets for the existing one.

In St. Petersburg, now renamed Leningrad, the great champion in the fight was a remarkable woman Agrippina Vaganova. This was her home town. She was born here in 1869 and had graduated from the Imperial school in 1897, only a year or so

before Pavlova, Trefilova and Egorova. Unlike her fellow pupils, however, her career moved very slowly. Although she developed a magnificent technique, one vital ingredient was missing: she lacked the personal charisma that draws an audience. It was not until 1915 that she was appointed ballerina, by which time she was 36 years old and nearing the end of her dancing life. But her new and far more important career was about to begin.

She started teaching at the Leningrad school in 1921 and brought total dedication to her task. Slowly and painstakingly she evolved a system of teaching that managed to blend harmoniously the best of the teaching that had gone before with the ideas of contemporary Soviet choreographers. It was an astonishing achievement and for the rest of her life she never stopped working to perfect it.

Her artistic reward came when the first generation of Vaganova-trained dancers graduated from the school – headed by a brilliant trio, Marina Semyonova, Natalia Dudinskaya and, perhaps the greatest of all, Galina Ulanova.

Natalia Dudinskaya, born in 1912, was another of the great Vaganova trained ballerinas, especially admired for her spectacular technique. She is seen here as Nikia in Act I of *La Bayadère*. (*Novosti Press Agency*)

Marina Semyonova, born in St Petersburg in 1908, trained with Vaganova, and became one of her most famous pupils. She was *prima ballerina* of the Bolshoi Ballet in Moscow from 1930–1952. This picture of her as Odette in *Swan Lake* was taken about 1934. (*Novosti Press Agency*)

Nor was it only ballerinas. Vaganova's system of teaching had a powerful influence on the development of the male dancers, for it taught them to achieve such complete control over their bodies that, with effortless technique at their command, they were able to project themselves fully into any role in the same way that an actor does. Dramatic realism was the order of the day and Vaganova's teaching was exactly fitted to it.

Throughout all these early years Vaganova continued to defend classical ballet against its attackers. Finally, in 1927, the state rewarded her loyalty and appointed her assistant director of GATOB

(Russian initials for the State Academic Theatre for Opera and Ballet). This was the transitional name from the old Maryinsky to the present-day Kirov Theatre. In 1931 she became its director and continued teaching until her death in 1951; since then she has been honoured by having the Leningrad Choreographic School named after her.

Meanwhile, in Moscow the Bolshoi ballet also had its battle for survival. The champion here was Alexander Gorsky, a Maryinsky-trained dancer who had gone to Moscow in 1900. He wanted to break away from the old Petipa system of mime, which had turned into a formal sign language, and wanted dancers to act their roles. His ideas were enthusiastically received by the young Bolshoi

Vassili Tikhomirov with his wife Yekaterina Geltzer dancing in Gorsky's ballet *Dance Dream*, when they came to London in 1911. (*Novosti Press Agency*)

dancers, and Gorsky had the opportunity to restage and revitalize many of the classics on this basis. He remained faithfully at his post as leading dancer and stage manager of the Bolshoi through all the turmoil of war and revolution. He fought courageously for the survival of the theatre and, when it finally reopened in 1920, he was made director.

Mordkin, who had been director for a short time before him, had left but Gorsky had a loyal supporter in Vassili Tikhomirov, who was one of the Bolshoi's leading dancers and, more important, one of their top teachers. When Gorsky died in 1924, Tikhomirov took over as director of the theatre and the school. It was he who produced the first Soviet classical ballet *The Red Poppy* which had its premiere in Moscow in June 1927. It was a full-length work with a plot of pure propaganda, set in contemporary China.

The beautiful dancer Tao-Hoa and her friends

Romeo and Juliet, first produced at the Bolshoi Theatre in 1946, has been one of the Soviet's most outstandingly successful ballets. It was created by Leonid Lavrovsky, the Bolshoi's ballet master, and a choreographer of rare talent. (*Novosti Press Agency*)

RIGHT Mikhail Lavrovsky, son of the great choreographer, in the Bolshoi production of *Swan Lake*. The hallmark of his dancing is his exquisite technique coupled with his dynamic temperament and great power of dramatic projection. (*Mike Davis Studios, Jesse Davis*)

Vladimir Vasiliev of the Bolshoi in *Spartacus*, the ballet based on the story of the slave uprising against the Romans and danced to music by Khachaturian. (*Mike Davis Studios, Jesse Davis*)

are exploited by the wicked capitalist Li-Shan-Fu. There is an uprising of coolies who are helped by their Russian comrades, the sailors of a merchant ship bringing grain for the people, and Tao-Hoa saves the life of the captain. Tikhomirov did much of the choreography for this ballet and his wife Yekaterina Geltzer created the leading role. *The Red Poppy* established the victory of classical ballet and became a regular favourite in the repertoire.

With the state now solidly behind it, ballet training was reorganized under the supervision of Vaganova whose system was made compulsory for all ballet teaching in the Soviet Union. After 1945 this order was extended to most of the other countries in the Eastern European bloc. Today there are nineteen training schools all over the Soviet Union, each following the detailed syllabus laid down by Moscow and Leningrad.

A child's training begins at 10 years old, after three years in a normal primary school. It is an eight-year course covering the usual academic subjects with the addition of music, history of art

The Red Poppy, 1927, was the first Soviet classical ballet, created by Tikhomirov who was, by then, Director of the Bolshoi. The sailors' dance, based on traditional Russian folk dancing, always stopped the show. (*Novosti Press Agency*)

and ballet. The dancing training covers classical ballet, character dancing and mime.

The Soviet system not only teaches the pupils, it also trains the teachers who have to go through a two-year course in Moscow or Leningrad to qualify and, for top teachers, there is a four-year university-type course leading to the Ballet Master's Faculty. More than this, the Method Department of the Moscow school keeps a close check on teaching standards, and organizes regular seminars and lectures. Every four years a grand seminar is held for representatives of all the schools to discuss and evaluate their work.

The result has been a stream of superbly trained dancers who rank among the finest performers in the world. It is interesting, however, that in spite of the centralized teaching system, the individual element has not disappeared. The Kirov and the Bolshoi have never lost their separate identities.

The hallmark of the Kirov dancers is lightness, pure line and great musicality. There is an aristocratic grace about their movements which gives a special quality to their productions of the classics. Bolshoi dancers are more dynamic and athletic and excel in the dramatic and the spectacular.

The Kirov continued to be the top company right through the 1920s and '30s and in Ulanova they had a ballerina who was the embodiment of everything they stood for. Her childhood went back to the old Maryinsky days when her mother was a dancer, and so the 6-year-old Ulanova had a glimpse of the ballets of the Tsars before the final curtain came down. Her first five years of training were with her mother before going on to Vaganova for the last four years before graduation. Like Fonteyn, she was never a dazzling virtuoso; the quality of her dancing lay in its lyrical beauty and her own personal appeal. On stage, sincerity and warmth seemed to radiate from her and she had the

Galina Ulanova, born in St. Petersburg in 1910 the daughter of two top dancers of the Maryinsky company, was trained first by her mother and then by Vaganova. She became *prima ballerina assoluta* of the Bolshoi Ballet, and a legendary figure to western audiences when she appeared with the company in the European capitals during the '50s. She is seen here in one of her most famous roles as Juliet, with Alexander Lapauri as Paris in *Romeo and Juliet* at the Bolshoi in Moscow. (*Novosti Press Agency*)

rare gift of being able deeply to move her audience. Like Pavlova, she became a legend in her own lifetime and western audiences, who were lucky enough to have a glimpse of her in the late '50s before she retired, saw unforgettable artistry.

In the 1920s, Ulanova, at the start of her career, was not only bringing the classics to a new generation of ballet-goers, but appearing in such sturdy Soviet epics as *The Flame of Paris* (1923). This is set in revolutionary France of 1792, when the people of Marseilles march to Paris behind their leader, Philippe and storm the royal palace of the Tuilleries.

In 1934 she was creating the leading role in a new ballet *The Fountain of Bakhchisaray*, based on a poem by Pushkin. The ballet tells the romantic story of a Polish princess Maria, who is abducted by the tartar Khan Girei and is stabbed to death by her jealous

Maya Plisetskaya in *The Little Humpbacked Horse*. The original ballet had been created for the Maryinsky company by Saint-Léon in 1864. Based on Russian folklore, it was an immediate success and has remained popular ever since, being constantly produced in various versions. This production was at the Bolshoi Theatre in 1969. (*Novosti Press Agency*)

the music of Prokofiev. This has been ranked as one of his greatest works. He captured the poetry and depth of meaning of the play through the dance and, in Ulanova and her partner Konstantin Sergeyev, he had two perfect interpreters of the leading roles. This ballet has not only won acclaim in the Soviet Union, but in the western world also.

For the Kirov this, sadly, was the last of their great ballets. The following year the Russians found themselves caught up in World War II as the Germans invaded their country. Theatres were closed and both ballet companies and their schools were evacuated. The Kirov were sent to Diaghilev's home town of Perm where they remained until 1944. Leningrad came under a long siege and the theatre was badly damaged by shellfire. By the time it reopened they had lost their beloved ballerina for Ulanova had been transferred to the Bolshoi.

This was the beginning of the shift of leadership to the Soviet capital. The Bolshoi now began to collect the top talent as the most promising dancers were directed there. One of the new young ballerinas was Maya Plisetskaya, who graduated in 1943. She was a dancer with a dazzling technique and also a powerful actress, starring in the film *Anna Karenina* in 1968.

Maya's heritage of talent was linked to a fascinating family network of dancers and actors. Her brother Alexander, who danced with the Bolshoi until 1970, went on to become ballet master in Peru. Her older brother Azari went to Cuba, where he became Alicia Alonso's favourite partner. All three were the children of an actress of silent screen days Raisa Messerer, whose sister, Sulamith and brother Asaf, were big names in the Bolshoi in the 1930s and '40s. Asaf also won fame as a teacher, and dancers from all over the country came to his *classes de perfectionnement*. He evolved a method of teaching that developed all the muscles gradually so that a dancer was safeguarded from the dreaded risk of sudden injury. His sister Sulamith also became a teacher in the Bolshoi where her son Mikhail was a dancer until their defection in Japan in 1980.

The superb Bolshoi dancers were first seen in Europe in 1956 when they also came to London for a season at Covent Garden. They caused a sensation. The company had a similar triumph when

rival. The fountain, from which the water falls like tear drops to the ground, is erected to her memory by the heart-broken Khan. Ulanova gave a deeply moving performance as Maria and the ballet was important as it was the first Soviet work to use a literary theme, although others were to follow.

A novel by Gogol was the theme for *Taras Bulba* in 1940, and that same year the heights were reached when Leonid Lavrovsky, one of the Soviet's outstanding choreographers, created *Romeo and Juliet* to

Maya Plisetskaya in *Raymonda*, a ballet originally created by Petipa in 1898 and constantly revived by both the Kirov and Bolshoi companies. She is partnered here by Nikolai Fadeyechev in a Bolshoi Theatre production. (*Novosti Press Agency*)

they visited New York for the first time in 1959. Since then both the Bolshoi and the Kirov have made regular world tours and their dancers continue to win world-wide admiration.

One of the less happy results for the Soviets, however, has been the loss of some of their finest dancers, who have transferred to western companies. This interchange has always been part of the ballet scene, but the Soviets see it as a political 'defection'. It cuts across their policy of isolation. Ballet for them, means Russian dancers, performing Russian ballets, to music by Russian composers, in a décor by Russian artists.

In theory there seems no reason why such a policy should not be successful in a country the size of Russia, but in practice it seems to have resulted in artistic sterility. No really great new works by Russian choreographers have appeared since the days of Lavrovsky, and by now the repertoires are showing signs of age.

Natalia Bessmertnova, born in 1941, graduated from the Bolshoi school in 1961 and became one of the company's top ballerinas. She is seen here in *Giselle* partnered by Mikhail Lavrovsky. (*Novosti Press Agency*)

For highly-trained, ambitious young dancers, this has inevitably produced feelings of frustration. They cannot fail to be aware that, through their art, they belong to an international network of artists whose creative sources are constantly renewed by a free interchange. It is hardly surprising, therefore, that for some of them, the pull of their great global heritage becomes stronger than the ties of home.

EASTERN EUROPE

Ballet in eastern European countries under Russian influence has developed along similar lines.

In Hungary the school that supplies the State Opera House in Budapest is based on the Vaganova system, though they have managed to keep some of their national identity through the work of their own great dancer and teacher Ferenc Nádasi, who was director of the state ballet from 1949 until he retired in 1962. Nádasi trained most of the present generation of Hungarian dancers, and recently they have opened up to western influence by including ballets by such choreographers as Ashton, Lander and Béjart in their repertoire.

Poland and its famous Warsaw school had to start

The Hungarian ballet company Sopianae rehearsing
The Cobweb. (John Topham Picture Library)

all over again after the holocaust of World War II
virtually destroyed their capital city. Leon Woizikovsky, who had left in happier days to join
Diaghilev, came back in 1945 to help his country by
teaching in the reopened school. Slowly the Polish
ballet rose from the ashes. In 1964 they opened their
new Grand Theatre in Warsaw and by the end of the
1970s ballet was flourishing once again, with five
state schools where Polish and Russian teachers
train the new generation of dancers.

Czechoslovakian ballet comes even more closely
under the Soviet shadow, as their state schools in

Prague and the other main cities are mostly con-
trolled by teachers from Moscow and Leningrad.
Their dancers so far have had few opportunities to
appear outside their own country, though recently
they won some awards in an international competition in Zürich.

Finland, which retains a precarious independence on Russia's doorstep, has had its own state
ballet company since 1921. Being next door to
Leningrad they have, inevitably, absorbed most of
the Russian ideas and the classical repertoire from
Petipa days, with the addition of more recent
Soviet ballets. The Finns' own choreography has
drawn heavily on the music of Sibelius, but in recent
years there has been a new surge of enthusiasm for

145

The National Ballet of Finland in *Gayané*, a ballet first produced by the Kirov company in 1942, and seen here in London in 1979. (*Mike Davis Studios, Jesse Davis*)

works by modern Finnish composers. Finland's geographical isolation has not helped the development of its ballet and, when they came on tour to London in 1979, they failed to arouse much enthusiasm.

Bulgaria has come onto the international dancing scene with its famous Varna competitions. Started in 1964 as a state sponsored venture, these have grown into a world-wide event of great prestige.

The competitions are held every two years at Varna on the Black Sea and dancers come from all over the world to compete for medals awarded by an international panel of judges. Apart from the prestige of winning a medal, it is a rare opportunity for individual dancers from both sides of the iron curtain to meet.

Dancers of the Hungarian ballet performing a *czárdás* based on national dances. The most famous examples of *czárdás* in ballet are in *Coppélia* and the ballroom act of *Swan Lake*. (*Mike Davis Studios, Jesse Davis*)

10
Denmark, Sweden and Germany

The magical name of Bournonville is synonymous with Denmark's unique ballet history, for August Bournonville dominated the Danish ballet of the nineteenth century, and continues to do so.

The story actually began a century before when the Royal Court Theatre was opened in Copenhagen and its first ballet master, the Italian Vincenzo Galeotti from Venice, arrived in 1775. He laid the foundations of the Royal Danish Ballet and started the school that continues today. He also gave the Danes their first sight of romantic ballet, and one of his most popular works still survives in their repertoire: *The Whims of Cupid and the Ballet Master* that had its premiere in 1786.

This is a light-hearted series of *pas de deux* by pairs of lovers from various countries. They go to a Temple of Love where they are blindfolded by Cupid, who is danced by a child. When they are released they discover that the mischievous Cupid has matched them wrongly and there is great confusion and hilarity as the lovers sort themselves out.

When Galeotti died in 1816 he was succeeded by the French leading dancer Antoine Bournonville. Trained by Noverre, he was a fine dancer, but he had no special talent for choreography and failed to give the company opportunities to develop. What he did give them, however, was his son August.

Born in Copenhagen in 1805, the boy trained with his father and went on to Paris to study with the great Auguste Vestris, followed later by two years dancing at the Paris Opéra. When he returned to Copenhagen in 1830 to take up the post of ballet master, it was this training and experience that shaped his whole technique and outlook.

Unlike his father, 25-year-old August Bournonville had all the talents needed for his new job. He was a brilliant dancer, a creative and imaginative choreographer and also a good organizer and teacher. He trained his dancers in the Vestris style and created more than fifty ballets for them, many of which are still danced today.

The Danish Ballet's production of *La Sylphide* which has carefully preserved the original Bournonville choreography since the Danish premiere in 1836. (*Mike Davis Studios, Jesse Davis*)

One of his first efforts was a version of *La Sylphide*, with fresh music by Danish composer Løvenskjold, in which he himself danced the lead, partnering his favourite pupil Lucile Grahn. The ballet has remained intact in the repertoire of the Royal Danish Ballet. Like *La Sylphide*, which is set in Scotland,

Fleming Flindt, who succeeded Lander as ballet master in 1966, appearing in a television recording of Lander's ballet *Festival Polonaise*. He is partnered by Harald's wife, Toni. (*John Topham Picture Library*)

many Bournonville ballets have a national flavour and one of the most popular is *Napoli*, that captures the gaiety of Italy.

The hallmark of a Bournonville ballet is its warmth and vitality. Curiously enough his efforts to make his ballets known outside his own country were never successful and it is only since his death that his international fame has grown, so that today a Bournonville ballet is a treasured possession in any company's repertoire.

When he finally retired in 1875 at the age of 70, he left a ballet company that was unique for it had remained untouched by the development of ballet elsewhere that had sent male dancers into eclipse. On the contrary, Bournonville male dancers have always tended to dominate the scene and their style is pure Vestris – light and bouncy, with superb precision and elegance. Denmark had preserved for posterity the French style of dancing that the French themselves had forgotten.

After nearly half a century the Danish ballet without Bournonville seemed unthinkable but his pupil Hans Beck took on the task and lovingly continued the tradition of his great master until 1915.

A company, however, cannot go on for ever living in the past. The Danish ballet needed a new sense of direction which they eventually found, after a long wait, under Beck's pupil Harald Lander, who became their director in 1932. He generated great creative activity as he developed a new repertoire, trained new dancers, introduced classes in the Russian style and took the company on its first tours abroad. He brought in leading choreographers like Massine to extend their range and his own works also made an important contribution. Among his best known ballets is *Études*, that had its premiere in 1948, and which depicts a ballet class of mounting excitement as the technique moves from basic barre work to a climax of spectacular feats of dancing.

The policy of inviting guest choreographers was carried on by Lander's pupil and successor Niels Larsen in the 1950s and '60s: Balanchine, Ashton, Roland Petit, Jerome Robbins and John Cranko all came to Copenhagen.

Since 1966 Flemming Flindt has been ballet master. He too is a Bournonville-trained dancer, concerned to keep the classical heritage alive, but he has also kept up the modern trend with works by Glen Tetley. Flindt's own choreography lies in this direction as well and one of his most original works, *The Lesson*, is based on Eugene Ionesco's one-act play. In the ballet a dance studio forms the crazy Ionesco world in which a dancing teacher becomes more and more demented over the work of his girl pupil and ends up killing her. The pianist, unmoved, neatly folds away her music and closes the studio; tomorrow the same thing will happen all over again.

Peter Schaufuss in *La Sylphide*. This fine young Danish dancer, trained in the Bournonville tradition, has built an international reputation both as a guest artist and as a choreographer. (*London Festival Ballet, Anthony Crickmay*)

ABOVE *The Lesson* was Flindt's first and most original ballet. Seen on Danish television in 1963, it subsequently had a stage production in Paris in 1964, and won the Italia Prize. It is now in the repertoire of many ballet companies. (*Mike Davis Studios, Jesse Davis*)

LEFT Erik Bruhn and Nadia Nerina in the famous Bournonville ballet, *Napoli*. (*Mike Davis Studios, Jesse Davis*)

OPPOSITE Niels Kehlet, a dancer of great virtuosity, with the Royal Danish Ballet in *Études*. One of the best-known works by Harald Lander, it was first produced in 1948, and is based on the increasing technical achievement of a ballet class. (*Mike Davis Studios, Jesse Davis*)

Since Denmark came into the mainstream of ballet, their dancers have been seen all over the world. Erik Bruhn was one of the first to go out, flying the Bournonville flag, and he has been called one of the finest dancers in the world. Peter Martins joined the New York City Ballet in 1969 and became one of their top dancers. Peter Schaufuss, another brilliant young dancer, was a silver medal-list in the Moscow Competition in 1973, and then spent three years with the New York City Ballet before going on to a freelance life, since when his star has been steadily in the ascendant.

SWEDEN

It was the Swedish royal family who were the founders of their country's national ballet. King Gustav III built the Royal Opera House in Stockholm in 1773 and his first ballet master was a Frenchman from the Paris Opéra. Modern ideas arrived in 1781 when Antoine Bournonville became ballet master before moving on to Copenhagen, and introduced Noverre's *ballets d'action*. He was followed in 1803 by the Italian Filippo Taglioni, who chose a Swedish wife, and it was their daughter Marie, born in Stockholm in 1804, who became the first of the great romantic ballerinas.

Swedish-born Jean Börlin in *Cleopatra* at the Paris Opéra in 1919. (*Stockholm, Collection of the Dance Museum*)

It was not until 1833 that the Stockholm company had its first Swedish ballet master Ander Selinder, who remained with them until 1856. Unfortunately he was not in the Bournonville class, and though he introduced some interesting folk dancing into classical *divertissements*, he did not contribute much to the general development of the company which came to rely more and more on neighbouring Copenhagen for its inspiration, and August Bournonville came to stage many of his own ballets for them.

Among the Swedish dancers of this period one great name emerged: Christian Johansson. Trained in Stockholm, and by Bournonville in Copenhagen, he was a *premier danseur* by the time he was 20. If Sweden had kept him he might have been another Bournonville, instead he went to St. Petersburg where Russia reaped the harvest of his great gifts. He stayed on to become head of the Imperial School of the Maryinsky Theatre and he is seen in ballet history as one of the main architects of the Russian school of dancing.

In the meantime ballet in Sweden went into decline. Interest in the dance was briefly revived when Fokine came to Sweden in 1913 and there were plans for him to take over as ballet master, but World War I put an end to this and he returned to Russia.

Fokine did, however, encourage the development of one outstanding dancer Jean Börlin, whom he trained in Copenhagen after the war. It was here that Börlin met the wealthy Swedish patron of the arts Rolf de Maré, which led to the formation of the Ballets Suédois in 1930 with Börlin as star soloist and choreographer. Rolf de Maré was aiming to rival Diaghilev in Paris by staging avant-garde works. He collected modern composers and artists to back up Börlin's prolific choreography and though they had considerable success it was not of a permanent nature. After only five years the Ballets Suédois ceased to exist, and none of their ballets has survived.

In Stockholm nothing of interest emerged until 1949 when British choreographer Antony Tudor was engaged to revitalize the company. He invigorated the school by introducing new teachers and gave the Swedes a new *Giselle*, as well as his own *Jardin aux Lilas* and *Gala Performance*, before taking off again.

It was British-born Mary Skeaping who, from 1953 onward, gave Sweden eight years of hard work. She brought with her the traditions of her Russian teachers Trefilova and Egorova and, in addition,

Isadora Duncan, high priestess of free-style dancing, with some of her pupils, in the early days. It was in Germany that she had her greatest success, and she opened her first school in Berlin. (*Mander & Mitchenson Theatre Museum*)

her experience of dancing in Pavlova's company and working as ballet mistress at Sadler's Wells. Although she was essentially a producer of the classics and built up a fine repertoire, she also encouraged young choreographers, among them Evo Cramer, who became director of the company in 1975. Among their top dancers now are Anneli Alhanko and her partner Per Segerström, who were silver medallists at Varna in 1972.

GERMANY

Unlike most other countries, Germany has no single national ballet; there are, instead, about fifty opera houses and ballet companies operating independently in the big cities. This is really a hangover from the time when Germany was divided into small states, each with its own ruler and its own court, which in turn meant that the development of ballet depended on the tastes and attitudes of a series of autocratic individuals, and their luck in picking the right ballet masters.

The Duke of Württemberg turned Stuttgart into a leading ballet centre in the eighteenth century by appointing Noverre as ballet master. Frederick the Great of Prussia put Berlin on the map in 1744 with his opera house and an Italian ballerina 'La Barberina', who was as famous for her love affairs as for her astonishing battery of pirouettes and *entrechats*. French ballet master Michel Hoguet and Paul Taglioni, brother of the famous Marie, dominated the scene in the nineteenth century and Berlin became an important centre for the leading dancers of the day when they toured Europe. Hamburg's ballet flourished in the 1860s under Austrian Katti Lanner and later, in the 1890s, it was Munich's turn with their ballerina, Danish-born Lucile Grahn.

It was Vienna, however, that gave Germany a ballet that was to become everyone's favourite: *The Fairy Doll*. Created by the ballet master of the court opera Joseph Hassreiter, it is the story of a toy shop in which the dolls come to life after the shop is closed. (The same theme was used by Massine in *La Boutique*

ABOVE *Cupid Out of Humour* is one of the very old Swedish court ballets revived by Mary Skeaping. She produced it at the Drottningholm Court Theatre in 1956. (*Stockholm, Royal Opera Ballet; E. M. Rydberg*)

LEFT Per Segerström and Anneli Alhanko, in *The Sleeping Beauty*. (*Stockholm, Royal Opera Ballet; E. M. Rydberg*)

OPPOSITE Evo Cramer's production in 1957 of the Diaghilev ballet, *The Prodigal Son*. (*Stockholm, Royal Opera Ballet; E. M. Rydberg*)

Fantasque.) *The Fairy Doll* had its premiere in 1888 and is still in the Viennese repertoire. It celebrated its 750th performance in 1973!

In spite of all this royal patronage classical ballet never really took root in Germany. Visiting stars were welcomed and applauded, but opera remained the important art and dancing was seen only as lightweight entertainment. The first real interest in the dance was aroused when the great opponent of classical ballet arrived – Isadora Duncan. Her powerful free-style dancing struck a responsive chord in her German audiences and she enjoyed her biggest successes there. It was in Berlin that she opened her first school in 1904. The school did not

Mary Wigman and her dance group in *Prayer*, one of her cycle *Songs of the Dance*, 1936. (*Mander & Mitchenson Theatre Museum*)

make much headway, but the Duncan ideas did for they linked up with other developments in Germany at this time.

The three key names in these developments are Dalcroze, Laban and Wigman.

Émile Jaques-Dalcroze was teaching music in Geneva when he began evolving a system to help his pupils develop a sense of rhythm. He taught them to translate sounds into body movements, and most of the movements he used were based on those of Isadora Duncan. It was not long before his idea spread as actors and dancers realized the value of his system and in 1910 he opened his famous school of Dalcroze Eurythmics at Hellerau near Dresden in east Germany.

That same year Rudolf von Laban opened his school in Munich. This Hungarian-born cosmopolitan had had a classical training in Paris, followed by mixed dancing experience with various companies. His main interest, however, was in the science and philosophy of movement and he began a detailed analysis of the relationship between movement, emotion and character, and evolved a working system to express this. It meant discarding classical technique and working out a whole new set of movements.

Into these two mainstreams of thought came a young woman with a powerful personality and a great deal of dramatic talent – Mary Wigman, who had been born in Hanover in 1886. She was 25 years old when she came to Hellerau and spent three years there absorbing Dalcroze's teaching of eurythmics. In 1913 she joined Laban in Munich and it was here that she created her first major work for her solo recitals. *Hexentanz (Witch Dance)* was performed without music. It was a powerful evocation of the violence of demoniacal forces; it was also Wigman at her best. Her intense dramatic projection and almost masculine strength came over with maximum effect.

She remained with Laban through the years of World War I when he moved his school to neutral Zürich and they only parted in 1919 when Laban went on to work in Nuremberg and Stuttgart, where Kurt Jooss became his pupil. Wigman herself went on with her solo recitals, and now her career really took off. This post-war period was the time when expressionism was sweeping through the arts, and it swept Wigman along with it. In 1920 she set up her own school in Dresden which became the centre of modern dance in Germany where free-style schools proliferated. Wigman herself continued to give dance recitals up to 1942 and her tours took in England and the United States of America.

While Wigman danced, Laban concentrated on his researches and theories. He worked as ballet director, first in Hamburg and later in Berlin, and during this time he evolved his now famous system of dance notation.

Since the days of Noverre and Feuillet, the problem of recording the dance had been tackled by various people. In Paris in 1852 Saint-Léon had worked out a code of pin figures; in St. Petersburg, Stepanov based his system on music notes, and it is thanks to his work that many of the Petipa ballets have survived. Laban brought in a new dimension by introducing time, and he developed symbols to indicate the duration of movement. His first book *Written Dance*, published in 1928, was the start of the world-wide recognition of 'Labanotation' as one of the most precise methods of recording movement.

Others have continued since then to make their contributions. In England, the artist Benesh developed his own system of notation that is used by the Royal Ballet, and the Israelis Noa Eshkol and Abraham Wachman have evolved a mathematical system that is popular with computer programmers. Possibly the final answer will lie with computers,

silicon chips and video tapes to build up libraries of the dance. In the meantime, Labanotation continues to occupy an important place and in 1979 the Laban Centre for Movement and Dance International in London celebrated the centenary of the birth of this great man.

The powerful thrust of the modern dance movement found its way into many of the ballets of the day, and it must have looked at one time like a serious threat to classical ballet. Free-style dancing, however, has its in-built limitations. It is difficult to teach successfully. With no inherited vocabulary of movement, pupils have only their own limited range to use, and tend to copy the mannerisms of their teachers. There are also no standards at which to aim.

The great natural dancers like Duncan and Wigman could overcome these limitations, but the lesser ranks of their pupils could not. Though the best of the free-style could compare favourably with

The Green Table, Kurt Jooss's best-known ballet, created in 1932, is danced here by a contemporary British company. (*Northern Ballet Theatre*)

John Cranko created this version of *Romeo and Juliet* for the Stuttgart Ballet company in 1962. His favourite ballerina Marcia Haydée is seen here as Juliet, partnered by the American Richard Cragun. (*Mike Davis Studios, Jesse Davis*)

RIGHT *Hamlet: Connotations*, by American choreographer John Neumeier, was created for the Stuttgart Ballet in 1976. Marcia Haydée is partnered by the Danish dancer Egan Madsen. (*Mike Davis Studios, Jesse Davis*)

Requiem, by British choreographer Kenneth MacMillan, was dedicated to the memory of John Cranko, whose sudden death in 1971 had been a shattering blow to the world of ballet. It was first danced by the Stuttgart Ballet with Marcia Haydée, Richard Cragun, Egan Madsen and Reid Anderson. (*Mike Davis Studios, Jesse Davis*)

classical ballet, much of it, being based on the individual and the mood of the moment tended to be ephemeral and dated very rapidly. After the 1930s the whole movement lost its momentum. It had, however, made a genuine and important contribution to mainstream dancing. Its vitality and sincerity shook the conventional foundations of classical ballet and gave new ideas to choreographers.

One of the first to try and blend free-style with classical ballet was the German dancer Kurt Jooss. He met Laban when he was studying at Stuttgart

159

and they became lifelong friends. Jooss, trained in classical ballet, studied Laban's ideas in depth and started putting them into practice when he formed his own company in Essen in 1928. It was here that he produced the famous ballet with which his name is forever associated, *The Green Table*, that had its premiere in Paris in 1932.

The ballet is a dance of death. It begins and ends with the futile discussions round the green table of diplomats at a peace conference. Inbetween it shows the horrific impact of war on the lives of ordinary people. The dominant figure of the ballet is Death, a role created by Jooss himself. He put into this ballet everything he had learned from Laban as well as his own best creative work, and it remains his masterpiece.

The Jooss ideas did not, however, find favour with the Nazis, and in 1933 he pulled out of Germany with his company to find refuge in England, where Dartington Hall in Devon became the base for the Ballets Jooss. At the outbreak of war Laban also came to England and set up his Art of Movement Studio in Manchester. This later moved to Surrey, where his pupil Lisa Ullmann directed it until 1973. Laban himself died in England in 1958. Jooss returned to Germany after the war and started up his school in Essen again where he did valuable work until his abrupt death in a car crash in 1979.

In the meantime, post-war Germany had been making a surprising U-turn back to classical ballet which was partly the result of the cultural invasion of the occupying forces. From the east came Soviet ballet, and from the west, English and American influences made themselves felt as touring companies arrived and theatres got going again, many of them with the help of their former enemies. Walter Gore, who had spent the war in the Royal Navy, came to spend three years in Frankfurt as ballet master. American Todd Bolender went to Cologne and Britain's Alan Carter to Munich.

It was Stuttgart, however, which carried off the prize. In 1961 the Württemberg State Theatre appointed John Cranko as their ballet director. This 34-year-old South African had been born and raised in Cape Town and came to England to finish training at Sadler's Wells, where his remarkable gift for choreography was quickly recognized. In ten action-packed years, Cranko built up the Stuttgart ballet from a provincial troupe to an internationally acclaimed company. He brought with him his favourite ballerina, Brazilian born Marcia Haydée, who created most of the leading roles in his ballets. Cranko's choreographic range and output were enormous and his sudden death during a flight in 1973 was a shattering blow. His place was taken briefly by Glen Tetley, but since 1976 the artistic direction has been in the hands of Marcia Haydée.

Post-war Berlin ended up with three ballet companies. East Berlin has the original Opera House with Soviet-style ballets, and also the East Berlin Comic Opera House, which is making a name for itself under Tom Schilling's direction. The trend here is towards modern dance. The West Berlin Opera House was rebuilt in 1961, and Kenneth MacMillan came out from England to become its director. He started out with some very fine ballets but had, unfortunately, to leave after only three years to take over the Royal Ballet in London, since which time there has been a succession of directors.

Contemporary dance and classical ballet are still battling for supremacy in many of the German opera houses. Cologne is in the forefront of the modern dance trend. Hamburg, Düsseldorf and Munich are among the leading companies with wide-ranging international repertoires.

Though it may look much like the same mixture as before, ballet in Germany is now established on a much broader basis, and shows every sign of becoming a very vigorous home-grown plant.

11

Australia

The other side of the world had its first glimpse of modern ballet only when Adeline Genée came to Melbourne with a company of Russian dancers in 1913. But, as had happened so often before, it was the magic of Pavlova that sparked off the rush of little girls to the dancing schools – and changed the life of one boy who, like Frederick Ashton, was to become one of ballet's great names.

In 1926 Pavlova and her company were dancing in Melbourne, and in the audience one night was a wealthy beef baron from South Australia. After the performance he went round backstage to find Pavlova and suggested that his son should take lessons with her. An audition was arranged, the 17-year-old boy was accepted and taken on as an extra for the tour. So Sir Robert Helpmann started his dancing career.

Australia was to see Pavlova once more when she returned in 1929. She was by then 48 years old and, though the legendary ballerina still had the power to enchant her audiences, her technique was not what it had been. The grinding years of hard work she had inflicted on herself had taken their toll of her physique, and she died two years later.

In the 1940s Borovansky produced a remarkable *Sylphides* with the professional company he had formed of home-grown, home-trained talent. (*Australian Information Service*)

The impetus that Pavlova gave to ballet was, however, soon being exploited by the keen-eyed entrepreneurs who ran Australia's biggest theatrical company, J. C. Williamson Ltd. They started in 1936 by importing Colonel de Basil's Ballet Russe. Box office takings were good, and from then on there were Russian ballet seasons each year when Australians saw the great dancers of the day, Lifar, Dolin, Lichine and the 'baby ballerinas'.

De Basil's 1939–40 season was the most glorious of them all but it was also the last, for Europe was plunged into war again and the era of the great Ballet Russe was almost over. Australia was never to see them again, but they had created a strong ballet-going public in the big cities. What next?

When de Basil's company sailed away in 1940, it left behind the man who would answer that question: Edouard Borovansky, known as 'Boro', who was to become the founder of Australian Ballet. This human dynamo from Czechoslovakia had been trained in Prague and danced as a soloist with the state company, he then joined Pavlova and had been with her on both her Australian tours. He found in this vigorous young country a spirit to match his own and settled in Melbourne, with his dancer wife Xenia, where he opened a ballet school.

These were days of tremendous opportunities in what was still virgin territory. Although there were a growing number of schools and a lot of amateur activity, there was still no professional company in Australia. Boro was to create the first.

He started by founding the Melbourne Ballet Club, putting on amateur shows whenever he could afford it, and from this grew the Borovansky Ballet Company, which was remarkable because it was dependent entirely on local talent. Though Boro could easily have found Russian-trained star dancers amongst those who were scattered about Australia, this was not what he wanted. Right from the start his aim had been for a truly Australian company, and he had a gift that amounted to genius for spotting promising raw material and training it. For the pupils it was a painful process as Boro was a tough disciplinarian and a highly-charged extrovert, generating violent reactions as he thrust his way forward. Steadily, remorselessly, he turned his

Prima ballerina Marilyn Jones dancing with her husband Garth Welch in *Illyria*, which was one of his earliest choreographic efforts. He was born in Brisbane in 1936 and was leading dancer of the Australian Ballet from 1962–74, going on to become artistic director of the Ballet Victoria. (*Australian Information Service*)

Corroboree, one of the first truly Australian ballets with choreography by Australian Rex Reid, was based on the tribal gatherings of the aborigines. Music and décor were also by Australians. The ballet had its premiere in Sydney in 1950, danced by the National Theatre Ballet. (*Australian Information Service*)

bunch of students into wholly professional dancers, while his brilliant showmanship kept this self-financed, struggling company afloat until their big break came in 1941 when they were taken over by the Williamson group. This meant access to the big theatres, top billing, and opportunities for young dancers.

Boro's showmanship produced good box office results for his masters and all through the war years they rode on the crest of the wave. The downward plunge came with peace. Everything relaxed, and the shrewd businessmen in Williamson's callously switched to a better potential moneymaker – musical comedy – so Boro's dancers, who were under contract, found themselves performing in *The Dancing Years* and *Gay Rosalinda.* Though Boro did manage to stage a full-length *Coppélia,* it was a final effort and in 1947 his company was disbanded.

It was not the end of Boro but for over two years he vanished into the wings.

Into the centre of the stage that year came the Ballet Rambert, newly arrived from England, on their first Australian tour, and bringing with them their leading dancers Walter Gore and Paula Hinton. Rambert took in some of Boro's most promising dancers, including 16-year-old Kathleen Gorham and 19-year-old Vassilie Trunoff who, in spite of his name, was genuinely Australian. In return, Australia acquired two of the Rambert dancers. Joyce Graeme had left them to take part in a move towards founding a national ballet, and when the National Theatre Ballet, backed by the Victoria state government, was formed in Melbourne in 1950, she became its first director. She was joined by her Rambert colleague Margot Scott.

Together they set about creating a truly Australian company, encouraging new choreography and design. A milestone was reached with Rex Reid's *Corroboree,* a ballet with an aboriginal theme handled with great skill and effect.

They did not have it all their own way, however, for the next year 1951, the indestructible Boro was in action again. He had pulled off a successful business deal with Williamson's and rounded up most of the members of his old company. Australia now had two professional companies.

For a time the rivals ran neck and neck. Then it began to look as though Melbourne's National Ballet were going to be the winners. After a very successful touring season they engaged the two

In 1951 'Boro', not to be outdone by his rivals, produced *The Outlaw*, suggested by the life of the legendary bush-ranger Ned Kelly. The story goes that Kelly, being arrested here by a police trooper, wore some form of armour plating to protect himself. (*Australian Information Service*)

Peggy Van Praagh came to the rescue of Boro's company after his sudden death in 1959. From this event grew the Australian Ballet of which she was the first artistic director and ballet mistress. (*Australian Information Service*)

leading Rambert dancers, Walter Gore and his wife Paula Hinton, to replace Joyce Graeme who had retired. 1951 was a tremendous season. It was also tremendously expensive. Future projects came up against the rocks of tough financial reality. There was a clash of personalities; the Gores did not see eye to eye with the business management and left, and the company, lacking an artistic driving force, gradually declined and finally ceased to exist in 1955.

Australian ballet was now back in Boro's hands. For him, though, time was running out, but he spent it laying the foundations for the future. He built up a solid classical repertoire, adding Australian works, including his own ballet *The Outlaw* based on the Ned Kelly legend. Choreography was the one item missing in the Boro package of talents and he was generally thankful to hand over this side of his company's activities to others. 1954 was a high spot when John Cranko arrived to stage the Australian premiere of his *Pineapple Poll*. Its great success was due in large part to Kathleen Gorham who, out of loyalty to her country, had rejoined the company at

Robert Helpmann's dramatic ballet *Elektra* tells of Orestes' return home ten years after his father Agamemnon was murdered by his mother Clytemnestra and her lover. It was first seen in Australia in 1966. (*Australian Information Service*)

the last minute to create the leading role, giving up the prospect of international fame. She was to stay with them for the rest of her dancing career.

David Lichine followed as guest choreographer, producing *The Prodigal Son* and his own *Graduation Ball*, that had had its premiere in Sydney in 1940.

The company also welcomed as guest artists two top dancers, Margot Fonteyn and Michael Somes.

By now Boro's company really dominated the Australian ballet scene and it looked as though nothing could stop them, except the one thing no

The premiere of *The Melbourne Cup* in Sydney in November 1962 celebrated the launching of the Australian Ballet. Here Elaine Fifield dances the debutante, Brian Lawrence the Jackaroo and Barbara Chambers the horse in the London production. (*London, Royal Opera House Archives*)

ABOVE Two great knights of the ballet, as two superb ugly sisters in *Cinderella*: Sir Robert Helpmann and Sir Frederick Ashton, whose brilliant performance in these roles have delighted British and Australian audiences. (*London, Royal Opera House Archives*)

LEFT Robert Helpmann as Dr. Coppelius in *Coppélia* in Sydney in 1969. He had become joint artistic director of the Australian Ballet with Peggy Van Praagh in 1965. (*Australian Information Service*)

FAR LEFT Marilyn Jones is one of the finest dancers ever produced by Australia. She is seen here as Kitri in *Don Quixote* in 1970. (*Australian Information Service*)

one had thought of. In 1959 the dynamic Boro collapsed and died of a heart attack just before the opening night of the new season.

The company were shattered, as Boro had been a one-man enterprise and had never trained an heir. They managed to keep going until, through the combined efforts of Ninette de Valois, Margot Fonteyn and Robert Helpmann, a replacement was found in Peggy van Praagh. Trained in Sadler's Wells and widely experienced, she was now free-lancing in Europe.

It needed a good deal of pressure to get a reluctant van Praagh to take on the job and the first season was not a happy one. The company were used to the Boro methods and did not take kindly to a new form of dictatorship. Box office takings plunged for the public had made up its mind that, since Boro had died, his company would die also. It did just that. The hard-headed businessmen of Williamson's were taking no chances on an unknown director so they organized the death blow for January 1961.

At their last performance Peggy van Praagh made a curtain speech announcing the end of Boro's company, and appealing to the audience to lobby their Members of Parliament for a government supported national ballet. The result was a backstage visit from a distinguished-looking, white-haired balleto-mane. His name was Harold Holt, and he was the Deputy Prime Minister of Australia.

That night the Boro ballet died, and the Australian Ballet was born.

It was not, in fact, a revived 'Boro' for other influences had been at work that were to give it a distinctive identity. It also took some time for the administrative details to be worked out but, finally, on 2 November 1962, to a great roll of publicity drums, the new Australian Ballet, under its director Peggy van Praagh, had its premiere at Her Majesty's Theatre, Sydney. *Swan Lake* was the main offering at the opening, but what really caught the headlines was the second night's programme featuring authentic Australia in *The Melbourne Cup*, a ballet about the one and only horse race in the world that rates a public holiday!

Soon after this, John Cranko brought a great addition to the repertoire with *The Lady and the Fool* to music by Verdi. The story tells of a wealthy young beauty La Capricciosa, who capriciously takes two poor clowns, Bootface and Moondog, to amuse her friends at a grand ball. Unexpectedly, she finds their performance touching and falls in love with one of them, rejecting her aristocratic suitors. The ballet was a mixture of spectacle and pathos and Australian audiences loved it. It is the only work that has remained continuously in the repertoire, with Marilyn Jones continuing to dance the role she created so enchantingly on the first night.

LEFT *The Display*, one of Helpmann's most outstanding ballets, had its premiere in Adelaide in 1964. The ballet centred round the mating dance of the Australian lyrebird. The spectacular costume was created by an old master-builder in London. The tail, measuring 5 metres across, is built on shafts of steel fixed to a parachute-type harness. Pity the poor dancer! In this picture it is Barry Kitcher. (*Australian Information Service*)

By now the new company was on its way. Artistically it was a success from the start. Financially, however, it needed a good deal of propping up, as its touring policy of visits to the smaller towns did not always pay dividends. A turning point came in 1964 when the company made its first appearance at the Adelaide Festival and caused a sensation with a new ballet created for them by Helpmann.

The Display is centred round the uniquely Australian lyrebird. Helpmann did a brilliant recreation of the bird's mating dance, building it into a complex

symbol of the frustrations of a woman who is dissatisfied by her lover, and by the stranger she meets. This was a Helpmann spectacular at its best and was a huge success.

That year, too, the company had a return visit from Margot Fonteyn with her new partner Nureyev. This was the first of several visits by Peggy van Praagh's ex-pupil, and his way of saying 'thank you' to her.

In 1965 the company came to London to represent Australia at the Commonwealth Arts Festival, and they brought with them to Covent Garden the famous *Display*. In this same year Robert Helpmann became much more closely involved with the company as he agreed to become joint artistic director. It was the start of a collaboration that was to launch the Australian Ballet as a company to be reckoned

The Australian Ballet presenting *Don Quixote*, 1972. (*Australian Information Service*)

The Merry Widow follows the plot of Lehár's operetta, and is danced to his music. Lucette Aldous and John Meehan are seen here dancing in the first production in 1975. (*Australian Information Service*)

RIGHT *Gemini*, a Glen Tetley ballet created for the Australian Ballet, had its premiere in Sydney in 1973. (*Australian Information Service*)

with. Van Praagh was essentially a teacher, Helpmann was a showman; together they were irresistible.

After London came the Paris Festival where they carried off a first prize for their *Giselle* against competition from such companies as the Kirov. World tours became an annual event. The Australian Ballet were in Montreal for Expo '67 and they also did a tour of the Far East taking in Singapore, Tokyo, and Bangkok. Then came the conquest of America with the help of Nureyev, who produced *Don Quixote*, in which he himself danced the lead, and to which Robert Helpmann added lustre by playing the title role.

Australia had put itself on the international map. Their director, now Dame Peggy van Praagh, after eleven years of gruelling hard work felt able to retire. Her co-director, now Sir Robert Helpmann, followed soon after, making a superb exit with his last, spectacularly successful *Merry Widow* in 1975. The artistic directorship was taken over the following year by British-born Anne Woolliams, who had been John Cranko's close collaborator in Stuttgart, and she has played an important part in consolidating their success.

Although the Australian Ballet is the name known to the outside world, a great deal of activity has also gone on inside the country. Schools all over the states, with steadily improving standards of teaching, have been producing fine professional dancers, and there are opportunities for them in many companies, such as the Ballet Victoria, where Garth Welch is artistic director and young talent is strongly encouraged.

New South Wales has its Dance Company; Adelaide has the Australian Dance Theatre. In Sydney, contemporary dance flourishes in the Bodenweiser company founded by an Austrian dancer, while the Sydney City Ballet concentrates on programmes for children. Queensland and Tasmania also have their own companies.

Out of all this is emerging a style of dance that is growing away from the parental shadows of the Ballet Russe and the Royal Ballet to form its own independent identity that will give Australian ballet its full place in the sun.

12

Around the World

SOUTH AMERICA

Buenos Aires in the Argentine has become the great ballet centre in South America. Though the city did not have a professional company of its own until 1925 classical ballet had been part of its cultural scene for nearly a hundred years before that, brought by visiting companies.

It really started when the original Colón Theatre was opened in 1857 and a visiting company gave Argentinians their first sight of *Giselle*. Over the years other companies brought such classics as *La Sylphide, Esmeralda, Coppélia* and most of the best ballets circulating in Europe.

With the new century the pace speeded up, especially after 1908 when the present Colón Theatre was opened, and a company of about forty dancers was formed. These were mostly 'ready-made' dancers imported from Italy. They appeared in the operas and provided support for guest stars such as the great Preobrajenska, who came in 1912, and the Italian ballerina Zucchi, who appeared in 1916. That same year, Isadora Duncan arrived and Pavlova, too, dancing with her own company. The city was the scene of Nijinsksy's dramatic marriage in 1913 when Diaghilev's Ballets Russes came to the Colón. They returned four years later for a second season.

In 1925, when the Colón's company was reorganized, it was Pavlova's former partner Adolph Bolm who took charge of the new group, most of whom were now Argentinians. Their leading dancers, however, came from the United States – Anna Ludmila and Ruth Page, who had both been trained by Bolm. His first ballet for the new company was *Le Coq d'Or (The Golden Cockerel)*. This Russian fairy tale, based on a poem by Pushkin, had started life as an Opera-Ballet by Rimsky-Korsakov first produced at the Bolshoi in 1909. It was Fokine's sensationally successful version, however, produced

for Diaghilev's company in Paris in 1914 that had put it into the world repertoire. Fokine banished the singers to the side of the stage and gave all the main roles to the dancers, who carried the story along by a clever mixture of mime and dance. Many years later, when Fokine revived this ballet for de Basil's Ballet Russe, he banished the singers altogether, and this is the way modern productions usually present the ballet.

Nureyev partnering the Argentinian ballerina Olga Ferri as Aurora in *Sleeping Beauty* at the Colón Theatre in Buenos Aires. *(Jorge Fama)*

Two top dancers of the Colón Theatre, Ghislaine Thesmar and Michaël Denard in *La Hija del Danubio* (*The Daughter of the Danube*). (*Jorge Fama*)

RIGHT The Ballet company of the Teatro San Martin in Buenos Aires, which specializes in producing modern and controversial ballet, is seen here in *Memorias*. (*Jorge Fama*)

Le Coq d'Or successfully launched the Argentinian company, and before long they were producing their own leading dancers, largely due to the teaching skills of Fokine's assistant British-born Esmée Bulnes, who remained with them for twenty years.

In the meantime, the leading choreographers of the day continued to come to Buenos Aires; Fokine, Nijinska, Massine, Lifar, Lichine and Tudor, all came to stage their own ballets at the Colón. The theatre was the base for Colonel de Basil's Ballet Russe during World War II and, in the 1950s, there were regular visits from the Marquis de Cuevas's company. Nureyev arrived in 1971 to stage his version of the *Nutcracker*, and also the *Sleeping Beauty* in which he himself danced, partnering the Argentinian ballerina Olga Ferri. The Russian tradition continued when Alexander Plisetsky, brother of the dazzling Maya, arrived from Moscow as guest teacher and choreographer.

So, over the years, Buenos Aires has attracted some of the finest dancers and choreographers in the world, while their own company at the Colón makes regular tours taking classical ballet to cities all over South America.

Dancers of the Mexican Ballet performing a ballet based on Mayan legend. (*Mike Davis Studios, Jesse Davis*)

Guest ballerina Maximova with the top Argentinian dancer
Basilis in Béjart's production of *Romeo and Juliet* at the
Colón Theatre. (*Jorge Fama*)

MEXICO

Once again it was Pavlova who triggered off this
nation's enthusiasm for ballet when she came with
her company for a three-month season in 1917. The
indomitable ballerina not only danced in conventional theatres, but also gave a performance in the
bullring where 30 000 people saw her and cheered!

Classical ballet took root, and Mexico came on to
the touring map of many famous companies.
Teachers began to arrive from Paris, the United
States and Russia, while a Mexican born teacher
set up her ballet school based on the London RAD
syllabus. Cuban teachers also influenced the training
of Mexican dancers.

Contemporary dance arrived in the person of
American-born Anna Sokolow, who had been
trained by Martha Graham and had danced in her
company, becoming one of the leading teachers and
choreographers in the contemporary dance world.
Sokolow came to Mexico City in 1939 and helped to

found the official government school of modern dance, out of which has grown the National Ballet of Mexico – a small company that concentrates on producing modern works with a definite national character.

Traditional ballet has had a more difficult time in spite of government help. Various independent companies were formed but did not survive for long, though individual dancers have gone on to achieve international fame. The government-backed, Ballet Clásico de México founded in 1963, was only partly successful and has, more recently, been re-formed as the new Compañia Nacional de Danza, with help from Cuba and Alicia Alonso.

Though the talent is there, Mexican ballet has still to find its own identity.

SOUTH AFRICA

This country has come into the ballet scene even later than most as it had no professional company until 1963. There had, however, been a great deal of ballet activity on an amateur basis for many years before then.

Schools had been under way since the beginning of the century. One of the first was founded in Cape Town by Helen Webb who trained such fine dancers as Maude Lloyd and Alexis Rassine. Teaching standards were kept up through the work of the Dance Teachers Associations founded in the early 1920s in Cape Town and Johannesburg, helped and encouraged by the Espinosa family.

One of the great pioneers at this time was South African-born Dulcie Howes. She had started her classical training with Helen Webb, gone on to study in Europe with such great teachers as Karsavina and Cecchetti, and danced with Pavlova's company.

Back in Cape Town she opened her own ballet school in 1930 and, two years later, started a performing group that evolved into the University of Cape Town Ballet. From this cradle of talent emerged many fine dancers and potential choreographers but, because there were no professional opportunities for them at home, they were forced to go abroad – mostly to London.

Choreographers John Cranko, David Poole, and Alfred Rodrigues found a launching pad for their talents with the Sadler's Wells Ballet, while dancers such as Nadia Nerina and Patricia Miller, also

joining the company, achieved an international reputation. After them, Johannesburg-born Monica Mason rose to join the leading dancers of the Royal Ballet.

In the meantime, Dulcie Howes fought steadily to raise her dance company to professional

Patricia Miller, a pioneer of professional ballet in South Africa, is seen here in 1969 in *Giselle*, choreographed by her husband Dudley Davies. She launched Durban's first professional company NAPAC, and though it is no longer in existence, the impetus of her work is still very much felt. (*CESAT, Human Sciences Research Council*)

Dawn Weller in *Papillon* 1979. The choreography for the revival of this romantic French ballet of 1860 was recreated by Ronald Hynd for PACT. (*CESAT, Human Sciences Research Council*)

standards. Her reward came at last in 1963 when the government woke up to the idea of subsidizing the arts and gave her a small grant which financed the appointment of a ballet master and soloists. Two years later the company became fully professional and was renamed CAPAB, after the Cape Performing Arts Board. Dulcie Howes remained as its director until 1969 when she retired and her pupil David Poole, back home again, took over.

Government finance also came to the rescue of struggling amateur companies in Johannesburg leading to the creation of PACT – the Performing Arts Council of the Transvaal.

In 1969 Durban launched its professional company NAPAC – the Natal Performing Arts Council, directed by Patricia Miller, also back home again, and her husband Dudley Davies who choreographed many ballets for the company.

Liane Lurie and Bruce Simpson with PACT in *Cinderella* 1979. This production was by one of South Africa's leading choreographers, Alfred Rodrigues. (*CESAT, Human Sciences Research Council*)

So the outward flow of talent has been re-channelled into South Africa's three fine professional companies who are now able to reverse the trend and welcome guest artists from Europe.

ISRAEL

In the days of Palestine under the British mandate, a Russian ballerina Rina Nikova came to Tel-Aviv, set up a school of classical ballet, and also started a performing group with her students. From this she evolved the idea of creating Biblical ballets combining classical dance techniques with Hebrew and Yemenite traditions of dancing. In 1933 Nikova formed the Biblical Ballet. It was only partly successful as there was a great deal of opposition to classical ballet at the time on the grounds that it was out of place in a young pioneering country. It did, however, float a balloon for the future.

Ann Layfield and John Simons in Veronica Paeper's ballet, *John the Baptist*, 1972 for CAPAB. (*CESAT, Human Sciences Research Council*)

In the meantime, a powerful trend of modern dancing developed in Tel-Aviv. This gathered momentum during the 1930s when a great exodus of Jews from Nazi Germany began arriving, for they brought with them the Wigman/Laban ideas of expressionist dancing that were then sweeping central Europe. This caught the mood of the Israelis and made a powerful impact. Before long it was being interwoven with the mixed strands of their own Hebrew, Arab, and oriental dancing traditions. Various groups formed, flourished briefly, and vanished; one, however, survived. This was the Inbal Dance Theatre, founded in Tel-Aviv in 1949 by Sara Levi-Tanai, who was a choreographer and songwriter of Yemenite stock. Her original idea was to preserve the songs and dances of her own people. Later, however, traditional Jewish culture was introduced with the poetry and music of modern Israel.

This company was the first successfully to merge modern technique with oriental styles and it made an immense artistic impact. The dancers, however, remained untrained until a fresh tide of visitors and settlers surged in during the 1950s when the newly formed state of Israel opened its doors to all Jews. These new arrivals, coming mostly from the United States, brought the American ideas of disciplined training for dancers. As a result, the Inbal company soon rose to fully professional standards and, by 1957, had become strong enough to take its art on tour to London and New York.

Among the visitors at this time was Anna Sokolow, who had done so much for contemporary dance in Mexico. Her first visit in 1953 was the start of a long and close association. She brought to Israel the experience and authority of her teaching skill, plus the fine artistry of her choreography. She staged many of her own works here, with a group that she formed – the Lyric Theatre. So, another thread was added to the complex wave of the emerging pattern of the Israeli dance.

Standards improved, but there was always a hampering lack of money until, in 1964, good fortune arrived when Bat Sheva de Rothschild came to settle in Israel. She had been Martha Graham's patron in America, and she now formed the Bat Sheva Dance Company in Tel-Aviv, with Graham as its first artistic adviser. The company, trained to high professional standards, has built up a fine repertoire of contemporary works by the leading choreographers and tours extensively. It is now backed by the government.

In 1967, Bat Sheva de Rothschild extended her patronage to the classics by founding the Bat Dor Dance Company. Actually, *Bat Dor* means 'contemporary', but the purpose was to give opportunities for young talent to dance in contemporary works based on classical as well as modern technique. The idea succeeded. The Bat Dor company rapidly established itself in Israel, and went on to build up an international reputation with world-wide tours. Its future would also seem to be assured as its school, established at the same time, provides training for some six hundred dancers.

Although the main trend in Israel has been towards modern dance, conventional classical ballet has now found a foothold also. The Israel Classical Ballet Company, founded in 1967, has won a loyal following.

Israel has, in fact, absorbed most of the main dancing trends of the western world and used them as a powerful means of expressing its own national identity.

CHINA

It was the Russians who brought classical ballet to Peking in the 1950s when teachers arrived from the Bolshoi and Kirov companies and set up schools. The Peking Dance School was started in 1954, and the Shanghai Dance School in 1960. Soviet ballet companies also became regular visitors, though the Chinese did also have occasional glimpses of western dancers such as the Ballet Rambert.

Since political tensions between Russia and China severed these cultural links, Chinese ballet has developed independently. Two main companies were formed: the China Dance Drama Troupe, based on Peking, and the Shanghai Dance School. Though some of the ballets in their repertoire are derived from western sources (the Peking dancers were seen briefly on British television recently dancing Hans Christian Andersen's tale of *The Little Match Girl*), most of their works are based on national revolutionary themes. Some have been filmed and shown in the west.

China's own dance tradition is essentially acrobatic and forms an integral part of opera, which also has its own complicated vocabulary of mime and gesture. This centuries-old style of dancing has now found its way into the new companies, giving Chinese ballet a distinctive national flavour, a combination of traditional and classical elements.

JAPAN

Nearly two thousand years of dance, based on religion, culture and history had evolved into a highly stylized technique before Japan came into contact with Europe's classical ballet at the beginning of this century. Their first real enthusiasm for it, however, was sparked off by – Pavlova! She came to Tokyo in 1921.

Four years later, modern dance arrived with the Denishawn Dancers from America, followed by

The Tokyo Ballet Company recently staged a stunning production in London of Balanchine's *Palais de Cristal*, usually called *Symphony in C*. (*Mike Davis Studios, Jesse Davis*)

Ruth Page and her company in 1926. These modern dance ideas were the first to catch on. During the 1930s the Japanese enthusiastically adapted this style of dancing to their own culture. Classical ballet did not really get going until after World War II, when a whole crop of schools and semi-professional groups sprang up. None of them, however, survived long enough really to establish itself.

Contemporary dance also continued to develop in the same somewhat sporadic manner. At the last count there were about fifty assorted companies in existence all over the country. Tokyo, however, continues to be the main dance centre, dominated by the Tokyo Ballet Company that was founded in 1960. It was shaped to a great extent by Russian teachers and choreographers, and it is now a fully professional group with a solid repertoire of classical and contemporary work. The company tours regularly, and was last seen in Britain in 1975.

So, ballet has gone round the world. There is by now scarcely a country that has not been in contact with it, even if only through the television screen. In those countries where it has taken root it has been enriched by the influence of national dancing traditions.

Like the spoken language that lives and grows through the minds of the people who use it, the vocabulary of the ballet, constantly absorbing new ideas, is strengthened and revitalized in its power to communicate. It is indeed a universal language of music, movement and colour, that transcends national barriers and links ballet lovers everywhere.

The Asami Maki Classical Ballet dancing a ballet based on a traditional lion-mask dance with Yoko Shimitzu and Toshihiko Fujiki in the leading roles. (*Mike Davis Studios, Jesse Davis*)

Chronology

17th Century

1635 Louis XIV, aged 15, dances as the Sun in *Le Ballet de la Nuit*
Lully appointed Master of the Royal Music
1664 Molière's first comédie-ballet, *Les Fâcheux*
1672 Foundation of L'Académie Royale de la Musique
Pierre Beauchamp appointed ballet master
1681 First appearance of female dancers at Paris Opéra

18th Century

1700 First book on dance notation published, *Choreography or the Art of Describing the Dance* by Feuillet
1713 School of dance established at Paris Opéra, financed by the state
1726 Marie Camargo makes her début at the Paris Opéra
1727 Marie Sallé makes her début at the Paris Opéra
1738 First ballet school founded in St Petersburg
1748 Gaetan Vestris makes his début at the Paris Opéra
1760 Noverre engaged as ballet master in Stuttgart
Noverre publishes *Letters on Dancing and Ballet*
1772 Auguste Vestris, aged 12, makes his début in Paris
1773 Royal Opera House, Stockholm, opened and ballet company formed
1776 Noverre appointed ballet master at the Paris Opéra
1786 Galeotti produces *The Whims of Cupid* in Copenhagen
1787 Gardel appointed ballet master of Paris Opéra
1789 Dauberval produces *La Fille Mal Gardée*, at Bordeaux
Beginning of the French Revolution
1796 Didelot produces *Flore et Zéphire* at the King's Theatre London, introducing 'flying ballet' on wires, and tights

19th Century

1801 Didelot appointed ballet master, St Petersburg
1803 Filippo Taglioni appointed ballet master, Stockholm
1806 Death of Dauberval, aged 64
1808 Death of Gaetan Vestris, aged 80
1810 Death of Noverre, aged 83
1812 Salvatore Viganò appointed ballet master, Milan
1820 Pierre Gardel retires, and the Paris Opéra moves into its new theatre, rue Peletier
1828 Blasis's book *The Code of Terpsichore* published
1832 Premiere of *La Sylphide* with Marie Taglioni
1834 Fanny Elssler makes her début at the Paris Opéra
1837 Blasis becomes director of dancing school, Milan

1839 The first 'export' American ballerina, Augusta Maywood makes her début at the Paris Opéra
1840 Fanny Elssler begins her American tour
Johansson makes his début at St Petersburg
1841 Premiere of *Giselle* with Carlotta Grisi
1842 Death of Auguste Vestris, aged 82
1844 Premiere of Perrot's *La Esmeralda* in London
1846 First performance of *Giselle* in U.S.A.
1847 Marius Petipa makes his début in St Petersburg
1852 Saint-Léon publishes his system of dance notation *La Sténochorégraphie*
1862 Premiere of Petipa's *La Fille du Pharaon* in St Petersburg
1869 Petipa appointed principal ballet master
Premiere of his *Don Quixote* in Moscow
1870 Premiere of Saint-Léon's *Coppélia* in Paris
1877 Premiere of Petipa's *La Bayadère* in St Petersburg
1879 Death of August Bournonville, aged 74
1887 Enrico Cecchetti makes his début in St Petersburg
1888 Premiere of *The Fairy Doll* in Vienna
1890 Premiere of Petipa's *Sleeping Beauty* in St Petersburg
1892 Publication of *Alphabet of Movements of the Human Body*, Stepanov's book on dance notation
Premiere of Ivanov's *The Nutcracker* in St Petersburg
1893 Death of Tchaikovsky from cholera
1895 Premiere of *Swan Lake*, choreographed by Petipa and Ivanov, in St Petersburg
1897 Adeline Genée makes her début in London
1898 Fokine makes his début at the Maryinsky
1899 Anna Pavlova makes her début at the Maryinsky

20th Century

1900 Isadora Duncan makes her first appearance in Paris
1902 Tamara Karsavina makes her début at the Maryinksy
1903 Petipa produces his last ballet
1904 Isadora Duncan founds her first school in Berlin
1905 Fokine creates *The Dying Swan* for Pavlova
1907 Vaslav Nijinsky graduates to the Maryinsky
1908 Adeline Genée's first visit to U.S.A.
Nijinsky's sister, Bronislava, graduates to the Maryinksy Theatre
1909 Diaghilev launches his Ballets Russes in Paris
1910 Premiere of Fokine's, *Schéhérezade, The Firebird,* and *Carnaval*
Death of Marius Petipa, aged 92
Dalcroze opens his school of eurythmics in Hellerau
Rudolf von Laban opens his modern dance school in Munich

1911 Premiere of Fokine's *Petrushka* and *Le Spectre de la Rose* in Paris
First London season of Diaghilev's Ballets Russes

1912 Premiere of Nijinsky's *L'Après-midi d'un Faune* in Paris
Marie Rambert joins Diaghilev

1913 Premiere of Nijinsky's *Le Sacre du Printemps* in Paris
Fokine leaves the Ballets Russes
Nijinsky marries and is dismissed

1914 Massine joins Diaghilev
World War I begins

1915 Agrippina Vaganova appointed ballerina in St Petersburg
Denishawn school opened in Los Angeles

1917 Russian Revolution begins

1919 Premiere of Massine's *La Boutique Fantasque* and *The Three-Cornered Hat* in London

1920 Ballets Suédois founded by Rolf de Maré
Foundation of Royal Academy of Dancing in London
Bolshoi theatre, Moscow re-opens
Mary Wigman opens her school of free style dancing in Dresden

1921 Diaghilev's production of *The Sleeping Princess* at the Alhambra, London
Vaganova begins teaching at the state choreographic school in Leningrad

1923 Anton Dolin, Ninette de Valois, Serge Lifar join Diaghilev
Premiere of Nijinska's *Les Noces*

1924 Balanchine leaves Russia and joins Diaghilev
Premiere of Nijinska's *Les Biches* and *The Blue Train*

1925 Alicia Markova joins Diaghilev

1926 de Valois founds her school in London
Frederick Ashton produces his first ballet *A Tragedy of Fashion* for Marie Rambert
Martha Graham founds her school of contemporary dance in New York

1927 Premiere of *The Red Poppy* in Moscow

1928 Galina Ulanova makes her début in Leningrad
Premiere of Balanchine's *Apollon Musagète* in the United States of America
Doris Humphrey and Charles Weidman found their school of modern dance in United States of America
Rudolf von Laban publishes *Written Dance* introducing Labanotation
Death of Cecchetti, aged 78

1929 Death of Diaghilev in Venice, aged 57
Lifar becomes ballet master of the Paris Opéra

1930 The Camargo Society formed in London
Marie Rambert's Ballet Club formed in London

1931 Death of Anna Pavlova, aged 50
First performance by the Vic-Wells Ballet
Premiere of Ashton's *Façade*

1932 Ballet Russe de Monte Carlo founded by Colonel de Basil and René Blum
Premiere of Kurt Jooss's *Green Table* in Paris
Premiere of *The Flame of Paris* in Leningrad
Harald Lander becomes ballet master in Copenhagen

1933 First visit to U.S.A. of the new Ballet Russe
Marie Rambert opens the Mercury Theatre, London

1934 Margot Fonteyn makes her début with Vic-Wells Ballet
School of American Ballet founded in New York

1935 Premiere of de Valois's *Rake's Progress* in London

1936 Premiere of Antony Tudor's *Le Jardin aux Lilas*

1939 World War II begins
American Ballet Theatre founded in New York

1940 Premiere of Leonid Lavrovsky's *Romeo and Juliet* in Leningrad

1942 Death of Fokine, aged 62
Yvette Chauviré becomes star dancer in Paris Opéra
Premiere of Agnes de Mille's *Rodeo*

1943 Premiere of Lifar's *Suite en Blanc* in Paris

1944 Premiere of Robbins's *Fancy Free* in New York

1945 Ballets des Champs-Elysées formed

1946 Sadler's Wells Ballet move to Covent Garden

1947 Marquis de Cuevas buys up the Nouveau Ballet de Monte Carlo

1948 New York City Ballet founded with George Balanchine as director
Les Ballets de Paris founded by Roland Petit
Premiere of Ashton's first full-length work *Cinderella* in London

1949 Premiere of Petit's *Carmen* in London
First American tour of Sadler's Wells Ballet

1950 London Festival Ballet formed with Markova and Dolin
Death of Nijinsky, aged 61, after thirty years in mental homes

1951 Death of Vaganova, aged 72
Premiere of Cranko's *Pineapple Poll* at Sadler's Wells Theatre
National Ballet of Canada founded

1952 Merce Cunningham forms his modern dance company in the United States of America
Benesh notation introduced into Sadler's Wells school

1955 Ballet de Cuba founded by Alicia and Fernando Alonso

1956 Sadler's Wells Ballet becomes The Royal Ballet
First visit of Bolshoi ballet to Europe

1960 The Ballet of the 20th Century founded in Brussels with Béjart as director

1961 Dutch National Ballet founded in Amsterdam
Nureyev asks for asylum in France
Cranko appointed director of Stuttgart ballet

1962 Australian Ballet founded in Melbourne

1963 Ashton becomes director of Royal Ballet

1964 First Varna competition held in Bulgaria

1965 First visit of Australian Ballet to London

1969 London Contemporary Dance Theatre founded

1970 Makarova leaves the Kirov ballet for the West
MacMillan becomes director of Royal Ballet

1971 Début of the Dance Theater of Harlem in New York

1974 Baryshnikov leaves the Kirov ballet for the West

1979 Alexander Godunov, Leonid and Valentina Koslov leave Bolshoi ballet for the West
Death of Kurt Jooss, aged 78
Death of Léonide Massine, aged 84
First visit of National Ballet of Cuba to Britain

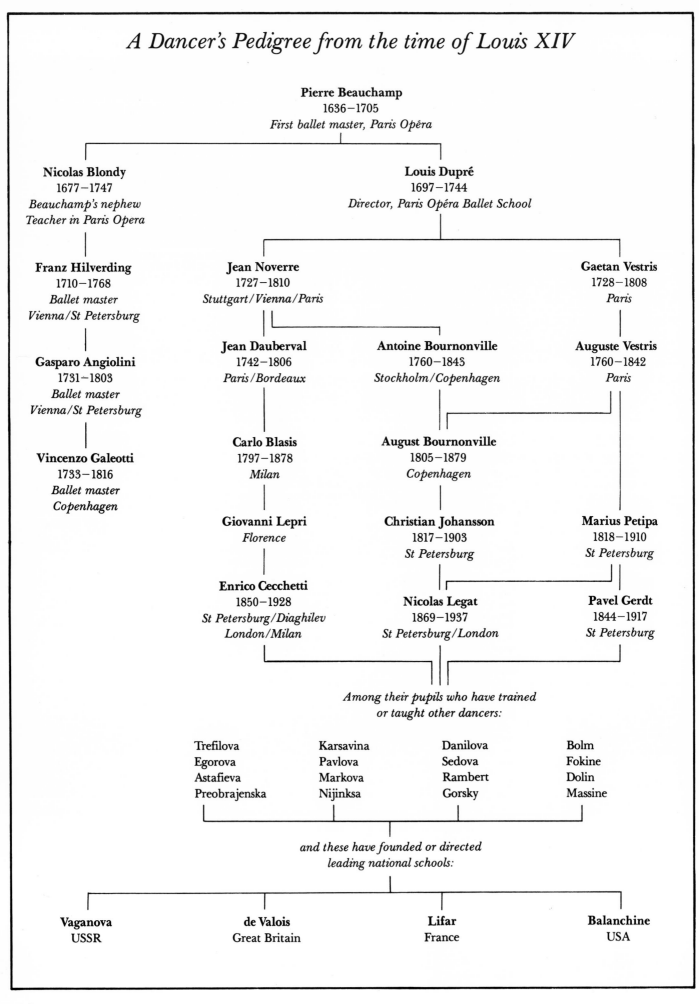

A Dancer's Pedigree from the time of Louis XIV

Pierre Beauchamp
1636–1705
First ballet master, Paris Opéra

Nicolas Blondy
1677–1747
Beauchamp's nephew
Teacher in Paris Opera

Louis Dupré
1697–1744
Director, Paris Opéra Ballet School

Franz Hilverding
1710–1768
Ballet master
Vienna/St Petersburg

Jean Noverre
1727–1810
Stuttgart/Vienna/Paris

Gaetan Vestris
1728–1808
Paris

Gasparo Angiolini
1731–1803
Ballet master
Vienna/St Petersburg

Jean Dauberval
1742–1806
Paris/Bordeaux

Antoine Bournonville
1760–1843
Stockholm/Copenhagen

Auguste Vestris
1760–1842
Paris

Vincenzo Galeotti
1733–1816
Ballet master
Copenhagen

Carlo Blasis
1797–1878
Milan

August Bournonville
1805–1879
Copenhagen

Giovanni Lepri
Florence

Christian Johansson
1817–1903
St Petersburg

Marius Petipa
1818–1910
St Petersburg

Enrico Cecchetti
1850–1928
St Petersburg/Diaghilev
London/Milan

Nicolas Legat
1869–1937
St Petersburg/London

Pavel Gerdt
1844–1917
St Petersburg

Among their pupils who have trained
or taught other dancers:

Trefilova	Karsavina	Danilova	Bolm
Egorova	Pavlova	Sedova	Fokine
Astafieva	Markova	Rambert	Dolin
Preobrajenska	Nijinksa	Gorsky	Massine

and these have founded or directed
leading national schools:

| **Vaganova** | **de Valois** | **Lifar** | **Balanchine** |
| USSR | Great Britain | France | USA |

Development of technique – *a few 'firsts'*

Pierre Beauchamp	*Ballet master, Paris 1669*	Said to be the first to classify the 'Five Positions' of classical ballet.
Mlle de la Fontaine	*1681*	First leading female dancer on the professional stage.
Marie Camargo	*Début 1726*	First female dancer to achieve *entrechat* 4, and to wear flat dancing slippers.
La Barberina	*Début in Paris 1739*	First to achieve *entrechat* 8.
Gaetan Vestris	*Début in Paris 1748*	First to develop the art of pirouettes at speed.
Anne Heinel	*Début in Paris 1768*	First to develop pirouettes for female dancers.
Carlo Blasis	*Director of dance academy, Milan 1837*	First to codify 'The Attitude' based on Giovanni da Bologna's statue of Mercury. First to publish a book on technique 1820.
Marie Taglioni	*1832 La Sylphide*	First ballerina to make use of points as part of a dancer's vocabulary.
Pierina Legnani	*1893 St. Petersburg*	First ballerina to perform 32 *fouettés*.

Index

Index of Ballets

FM 3/56

FM 3/56